Maria Suelene Dantas

Stress and Depression - From the Perspective of Body Psychology

Maria Suelene Dantas

Stress and Depression - From the Perspective of Body Psychology

ScienciaScripts

Imprint
Any brand names and product names mentioned in this book are subject to trademark, brand or patent protection and are trademarks or registered trademarks of their respective holders. The use of brand names, product names, common names, trade names, product descriptions etc. even without a particular marking in this work is in no way to be construed to mean that such names may be regarded as unrestricted in respect of trademark and brand protection legislation and could thus be used by anyone.

Cover image: www.ingimage.com

This book is a translation from the original published under ISBN 978-613-9-74839-6.

Publisher:
Sciencia Scripts
is a trademark of
Dodo Books Indian Ocean Ltd. and OmniScriptum S.R.L publishing group

120 High Road, East Finchley, London, N2 9ED, United Kingdom
Str. Armeneasca 28/1, office 1, Chisinau MD-2012, Republic of Moldova, Europe
Printed at: see last page
ISBN: 978-620-6-25139-2

"The prevention of armor would be unnecessary if our children could
develop as nature or 'God' has prescribed."

Wilhelm Reich

ACKNOWLEDGMENTS

If I were to list all the people who have helped me, I would certainly need to fill several pages. So I am very grateful to everyone who has been and is part of the story of my life.

But of all these people, I would like to thank in particular my parents who allowed me to exist. To my dear Jaime, for his enormous patience and support. To Allan, Natalia and Fernanda for the informal conversations, in person, over coffee, or through social networks, which greatly relieved my tensions. Thanks also to all the other people who encouraged me to write this book. And without a doubt, I must thank the precious contributions and notes of the loving couple: Jose Henrique Volpi and Sandra Mara Volpi, without whom I would not have known and experienced this wonderful science that is Body Psychology. To my patients, who give me a better perception of the human being, allowing my personal and professional growth. And of course, I cannot forget a great friend and inspiration in this adventure, Joana.

Love,

Suelene Dantas

PRESENTATION

Wilhelm Reich was the forerunner of body psychotherapies. He first focused his studies on the theory of libido, which played a central role n psychoanalysis. He treated psychic imbalances according to the proposal of psychoanalysis, analyzing neurotic symptoms and emphasizing the word and, gradually, he realized that the patient also expressed his unconscious contents through the body, through posture, tone of voice, clothing, etc. He took the patient off the diva and sat face to face with him, which allowed him to get in touch with the person on a level beyond that of the neurosis under treatment.

By better understanding the bodily reactions of his patients and based on these reactions, Reich developed a technique of intervention, which he called character analysis. Character analysis is a purely verbal work, but it already includes the body in the treatment, however, without yet touching it. This means to be clear about the patient's most striking and compromised character traits in order to be able to mature them, which in this case means to make the patient more aware of his behavior, gestures, postures, tone of voice, clothing, etc., and to relate this to the neurotic conflicts that disturb him.

Reich also found that psycho-emotional disorders are always associated with anatomical-physiological dysfunctions, which in turn are part of a unified system. This set of bodily dysfunctions was named muscular courapas, which are chronic tensions that form in the body throughout life, whose function is to protect the individual (ego) from painful and threatening experiences. From this, his work ceased to be a psychological therapy only and became a psychotherapy directly focused on the body, the neurovegetative system. For this reason, it was called character-analytic vegetotherapy, including in a single concept the work on the psychic and physical apparatus.

Reich proposed a psychotherapeutic approach where verbal analysis should be added to body and energy work. His intention was a form of psychotherapy that considers the body, mind and energy as a unit that should be treated as a tripe, jointly and indivisibly.

The purpose of this book, simple but profound, technical but didactic, is to lead the reader to know a little more about this fascinating work, which is part of Body Psychology, and its relationship with stress and depression. It is an invitation to venture both as a person and as a professional.

Jose Henrique Volpi

INDICE

1. INTRODUCTION

Have you ever imagined a sunny day, in a paradisiacal, exuberant place, where nature seems to invite you to bathe in the waters of peace and happiness? In such a place, you believe you would be privileged and would not let sadness be part of your life.

Unfortunately, even in such a place, there are people enveloped in an atmosphere of miasma, oblivious to the pleasurable moments that life can provide.

There is a popular phrase that says: "The sun rises for all". This makes us think that although we all have a life full of opportunities and subject ourselves to great achievements, we find people who cannot see these opportunities or lack the will to invest in their dreams to achieve success.

For some, life is wonderful, for others it is full of difficulties and heartbreak. While some people are able to face the bumps in the road, looking for ways to overcome obstacles, others write themselves off, give in to discouragement and frustration.

Each of us has a different view of life and its facets, with different reactions to the same problem or difficulty.

In this way, we can ask ourselves why we are so different from each other? Why do some manage to overcome certain difficulties, while others give in, letting themselves down, affecting their physical and mental health?

The way we organize ourselves in life, our way of functioning, can be better understood when we direct our gaze to human psycho-affective development. In this process, the child participates in constant and profound experiences with his parents. In this way, the interaction of the child with the environment can shape and change his perception, his way of looking and feeling life through a certain prism.

At this time of development, feelings and emotions play a major role in the formation of a person's character and personality, and if these emotions and feelings are disorganized, they can contribute to a diseased psychic structure.

So, before we talk about stress and depression, we should make some explanations, addressing some concepts, so that the reader can have a better understanding of these problems that affect millions of people, which has been growing in recent years, and have an understanding of what Body Psychology is. This science offers, in its postulates, a clear perception of what can originate this psychopathy (depression) and, through its therapeutic techniques, help to reverse this situation. In addition, it can act satisfactorily in the treatment of stress.

2. FEELINGS, EMOTIONS, PLEASURE AND DISPLEASURE

The feelings and emotions are directly linked to the quality and quantity of energies involved in the process of interaction of the subject with the environment. Reich (sd) comments that all this is linked to motility, which are the movements of the living organism to be expressed in a unique language, different from the language based on words, which we call the expressive language of the organism.

The feelings of love, hate, anguish, jealousy, as well as the emotions of anger, fear, joy, sadness, pleasure and displeasure are part of the experience of each of us, in our development process, from childhood to adulthood.

Lowen (1966) comments that consciousness develops as a result of our body's perception of the sensations produced by bodily activities. This perception is important for the regulation of behavior, that is, the effort to obtain pleasure and avoid pain. "Absence of sensation, whether motor or not, leads to disintegration of consciousness". (Lowen, 1966, p. 01).

For Reich (1978), the emotion of pleasure is a movement expressed at the plasmatic level, from the center to the periphery, while in displeasure, the unpleasant emptions cause a remotion, from inside to outside the organism. Pleasure and displeasure are related to the impulsive movements from the unconscious to the conscious.

It is human nature to seek the pleasure of living, something that may not happen when the individual is ill, but it is not always possible to avoid displeasure. "We have clarified the meaning of each of these two words: displeasure means maintenance or increase of tension, and pleasure, suppression of tension". (Nasio, 1995, p. 18). Thus, every effort used to achieve something or reach a certain goal, represents a displeasure, increased pressure. The moment this goal is achieved, or we get the realization of our desire, there will be a pleasure, the suppression of tension. "The feeling of pleasure is the perception of an expansive movement, as a flow of feeling and energy that goes to the periphery of the body". (Volpi and

Volpi, 2008, p.121).

Lowen (1977) states that emogao, in itself, means an outward movement, and that in higher organisms, this movement is synonymous with discharge, and that emotional crises are directly related to affective discharges. "Every bioenergetic change acts simultaneously on two levels. At the somatic level there is an increase in mobility, coordination and control; at the psychic level, a reorganization of thought and attitude" (Lowen, 1977, p. 115).

Damasio (1998) defines emotions as a combination of a process that goes through a mental evaluation, can be simple or complex, with responses directed and felt emotionally by the body and the brain. He says that emotions and feelings are fundamental for biological regulation, which establishes a bridge between rational and non-rational processes.

For this author, some feelings are related to emotes, but there are many that are not: all emotes give rise to feelings, if you are awake and aware, but not all feelings come from emotes. The author calls feelings without emotes background feelings. Feelings with emojis appear as sensations, i.e. they are felt by us, for example: in the acceleration of the heartbeat or in the movements of the intestine, among other sensations.

With this, we can infer that the emogogies appear in body movements, where the mind, our inner world, what we are and what we think, become physical axes unconsciously, experienced still in the first relationships of the child with himself and with the other. These emotions can be transformed into good or bad memories. Following this thought, the dynamic energetic process is already installed in the imaginary universe of the couple, from the moment their child occupies the place of desire of his parents.

Thus, in the process of human development, emotions and feelings are present from the moment of conception. From this moment, the embryo will receive an affective charge that can bring good or bad effluvium. These are loads of energies that will contribute to its development being healthy or disturbed, favoring or harming its psychic health. Faced with difficulties in elaborating unpleasant experiences, these emotions will be repressed, lodging in the unconscious, with returns often expressed in the body, without there being awareness of the somatic disorder. "With the growth and development of consciousness in the human organism, these sensations of pleasure and pain have been elaborated and transformed into emotions". (Lowen, 1966, p. 01).

According to Navarro (2013), the repression of the emotion will determine the energy block at the level at which the stimulus occurred, and that this block can be anorgonotic (energy deficiency) or hyperorgonotic (energy stagnation). Therefore, we will have a deficit energy, which decreases our daily actions; or a hyper-orgyony, an energetic reprehension, which accounts for psychopathologies.

Based on this, it is verified the importance of studying the stages of emotional development of the individual, because during these stages, energy blockages can occur, affecting the body and mind, leading to a compromise in the personality and character of the subject in his adult life.

Body Psychology has as its principle the understanding that body, mind and energy are inseparable, interacting dynamically, in a totality. It is based on the study of the stages of emotional or psycho-affective development, of the energies that circulate in the organism, of the energetic blockages, due to the developed courages. Within this approach, we seek to determine the couragas that have been lodged in the patient's body and, through the psychotherapeutic process, using specific techniques, stimulate physical and energetic movements, in order to promote the flexibilization of these psychological courapas, which have become physical, causing pain in the body, and to restore the normality of the energy flow, giving the patient back the dominion of the direction of his life.

3. BRIEF HISTORY OF BODY PSYCHOLOGY

The term Body Psychology was created by Dr. Jose Henrique Volpi and Ma. Sandra Mara Volpi in 1998. Fruit of the dedication and research of these characters, Body Psychology has its foundations in the works and studies of Wilhelm Reich, Federico Navarro, Alexander Lowen, among other collaborators, who contributed significantly to the construction of its principles and foundations.

Body Psychology, therefore, is a science that comprises the interaction of the schools of Reichian Analysis or Orgonomy (vegetotherapy or orgone therapy), Bioenergetic Analysis, Biodynamic Analysis, among others.

Without detracting from the work done by so many dedicated and studious people who have contributed to building Body Psychology, we will try to talk about the main authors who have brought the basis of its postulates.

3.1. WILHELM REICH

According to the Reichian Center (2018), the Reichian Analysis originated from the work developed by the Austrian physician Wilhelm Reich (1897-1957).

Reich, after years of research, decided to abandon the technique of psychoanalysis and devote himself to the study of body, mind and energy. He was the pioneer of Body Psychotherapy.

As a physician and psychoanalyst, he observed that the body keeps track of the history of each individual. At first, he encountered the difficulty of a large number of patients to find a cure, what we call resistance. He identified that this resistance came from the character of each patient and, with this, he directed his research to find ways to rescue the deepest emotions. In this effort, he was able to develop the technique of Character Analysis, unlike psychoanalysis which seeks to analyze the symptom.

The process of Character Analysis seeks to highlight the patient's emotions, which are expressed through their posture, way of speaking, acting, walking, etc.

After some time, Reich realized the existence of muscular tensions in various parts of the body, which he called courapas, and that these were linked to the individual's mind, his psyche. He mapped the body and named them in seven segments: ocular, oral, cervical, thoracic, diaphragmatic, abdominal and pelvic. With this new approach, he gave rise to Vegetotherapy, since the psychological is directly linked to the neurovegetative system. Each segment retains a particular history, resulting from stresses suffered during the stages of psycho-affective development, common to all of us, human beings, since gestation.

In this way, it seeks to relax the rigidity of the character, and also of the courapas, restoring biopsychic motility.

After some time, deepening his research, Reich observed a form of energy that circulates within us and that this energy is also found in the Cosmos. He called it orgone. He found that the concentration of energy can vary in different ways for each human being. This discovery led him to change the term from Vegetotherapy to Orgonotherapy. In this new form of analysis, the aim is to bring the patient into contact with himself and to re-establish the flow of orgone in his body. With this, there will be an internal regulation, that is, a regulation in the organic field. This self-regulation occurs as a result of the organization of the individual's thoughts and emotions.

3.2. FEDERICO NAVARRO

Federico Navarro (1924-2002), an Italian physician and neuropsychiatrist, was a student of Ola Raknes, a great friend and follower of

Reich. Raknes, in addition to transmitting to him all the knowledge of Reichian analysis, passed on to his student the task, which Reich had previously asked of him, of elaborating practical procedures that could be used on patients, the so-called "actings".

> Raknes had received from Reich the mission to systematize vegetotherapy and develop specific movements for the unblocking of each segment of couraga mapped in the body and passed this mission on to Navarro who, with his knowledge of neuropsychiatry and approximately ten years of psychoanalytic practice, brilliantly fulfilled the task. (VOLPI, 2000, p. 19).

Actings are expressive movements organized with the intention of awakening the organic functionality of the patient's body in the sessions of Reichian analysis. This technique works the seven segments of the armor, offering an activation of the neurovegetative system to unblock tensions in specific regions of the body. "Acting is not a mechanical exercise, gymnastics, as is commonly believed, but the proposal of an intentional dynamic action, which the patient performs with the involvement of his neuromuscularity". (Navarro, 2013, p.44).

His contribution was not limited to the construction of "actings". Navarro sought to demonstrate how the mind interferes with the body and the body, in turn, interferes with the mind, proposing a way to analyze the process of mind-body interaction, which he called Somatopsychodynamics.

> With the so-called Somatopsychodynamics, describing the philosophy and pathologies of the psyche in a systemic and evolutionary way, Navarro (1996b) further extended Reich's thinking, showing how the body can influence the mind and the mind, in turn, interfere in the energetic, bodily and emotional processes, thus forming a functional unity. (Volpi and Volpi, p. 119, 2008).

In addition, Navarro developed the types of character stipulated by Reich, differentiating character from characteriality, which are traces of character, which are directly related to body blockages, adding, also, the characteristic coverings that function as a defense mechanism.

3.3.   ALEXANDER LOWEN

Alexander Lowen (1910 - 2008) was a student and patient of Reich, first trained in law, and became a Reichian psychotherapist. According to Volpi & Volpi (2008), due to Reich's claim that medical training was necessary to work with psychotherapy, Lowen graduated in medicine from the University of Geneva.

Lowen returns to the United States and, imbued with new ideas, but in line with the theoretical foundations of Reichian analysis, associates himself with John Pierrakos, who also did Reichian therapy and was therefore a follower of Reich, together they found the International Institute of Bioenergetic Analysis.

According to Volpi & Volpi (2008), this new form of psychotherapy is based on some precepts, such as:

a) The essential goal of life is pleasure;

b) The human being is considered as a whole being - biological, psychological, social and cultural;

c) The biological energy that flows in the body is dynamic and causes well-being when its flow is in balance;

d) A balance between loading and unloading is necessary. Charge and discharge represents a cycle where the individual first feels the need, which makes him take action in search of satisfaction, with interaction of the body with the environment. When the individual has achieved what he or she wanted, there is relaxation;

e) Movement and breathing are key to increasing energy, providing self-expression and restoring the flow of bodily feelings.

Lowen (1982) defines bioenergetics as a therapeutic technique that helps the patient to connect with their body, which will help them to get the most out of what their body can offer. It also clarifies that this includes sexuality, but also the most basic functions of breathing, movement and self-expression. In this way, he states that: "the individual who does not breathe properly reduces the life of his body. If he does not move freely he limits the life of his body. If he does not feel fully, he narrows the life of his body, and if his self-expression is reduced, the individual will have the life of his body restricted" (Lowen, 1982, p. 38).

3.4. JOSE HENRIQUE VOLPI AND SANDRA MARA VOLPI

Dr. Jose Henrique Volpi and Ma Sandra Mara Volpi, directors of Centro Reichiano, were friends and students of Navarro. Dr. Jose Henrique Volpi was also his patient. They have dedicated their lives to research and study of the various schools of body psychotherapy. Based on these studies and therapeutic experiences throughout their lives, they formulated for Body Psychology the theory of the "Stages of Emotional Development", which contributes greatly to a better understanding of the stages of development that a child goes through, from conception to adolescence, which will influence the formation of his temperament, personality and character.

The term Body Psychology, which they coined in 1998, emerged with the publication of the first volume of the Body Psychology Journal. This is published annually by the Reichian Center.

According to Volpi and Volpi (2008) Body Psychology can be defined as a science that seeks to examine and analyze how the mind manifests itself on the body, and this in relation to the mind, starting from the assumption that the mind and body participate in a unique energetic movement, influencing the behavior of the individual. It understands that the human being must be analyzed as a whole: mind, body and energy.

> Body reading, investigation of personal history, understanding of character, massage and various other resources are used to formulate a diagnosis of character traits, energy and courages to create a psychotherapeutic work project that is individual for each patient (VOLPI and VOLPI, 2018).

In this way, Body Psychology aims to make the patient try to regulate their own energy, their emotions and their feelings, in order to provide good physical and mental health, with joy and well-being.

4. CHILD DEVELOPMENT PROCESS

In order to have a better understanding of the psychic disorders that affect today's adult, it is of paramount importance to understand the phases of their development, since, if there are failures in one of these phases, following the psychoanalytic precepts, it will cause a fixation, which will reflect on their psychic health, fostering, as an example, depression or melancholy (related to a fixation in the oral phase).

Fixation is when a child is unable to move through a stage satisfactorily. Their development is arrested at the stage where they felt secure and gratified.

Freud's concepts have contributed greatly to studies of infantile sexuality as well as personality formation.

> Freud conceived of personality development from the concept of libido. Libido is a biological concept and means the energy which is at the disposal of the life or sexual impulses. This energy comes from certain biochemical processes whose intrinsic dynamism is not yet fully known. It undergoes a process of development which takes place in a series of predetermined stages or phases. That is to say, all people, whatever their environment, will reach adulthood through a succession of phases in a practically inevitable sequence (D'ANDREA, 1994, p. 26).

Body Psychology, understood here as the set of various psychotherapeutic schools of the body, which have Reichian concepts as the basis of their postulates, brings a new theory and view of the human being, completing the contents of psychoanalysis. His ideas favor a new approach in dealing with the symptoms presented by patients, providing a look at the whole: mind, body and energy. In this context, we seek to research the entire life history of this patient, to determine how his psycho-affective development proceeded and, with this, help him to overcome the blockages that originated in this process.

4.1. THE CHILD IN THE VIEW OF PSYCHOANALYSIS - DEVELOPMENT OF SEXUALITY

The phases of the child's development take place, within the psychoanalytic theory, between the birth of the baby until the age of 6 and 7, according to the natural time of each one and how much it was stimulated in the relationship with another, in a positive or negative way. These phases are determined as: pre-genital (oral and anal) and genital (phallic, latency and genital).

In the oral phase, the erogenous zone and the mouth. Being fed and having the love of the other. This magical moment, which takes place in a bodily relationship between mother and baby, promotes an illusion of completeness, that is, according to psychoanalytic precepts, a narcissistic cell, where the baby feels the satisfaction of pleasure during the "feeding", with the affection that accompanies this dual moment, being seen by an observer and as if one really completed the other.

In the anal phase, sphincter control occurs. Expelling and retaining feces is related to exchanges of affection with the other. The child, having passed through the first moments in a satisfactory way, moves on to the next phase in a more harmonious way. The phallic phase, when the child realizes sexual differences, is the crucial moment of the Oedipus Complex. The triad (mother-child-father) develops an important influence on the child's psychic development, when he is faced with anatomical differences and the involvement of castration, and all the pulsional conflicts that involve this moment. In summary, we can say that in the boy, the fear of losing his penis appears and, in the girl, the envy of not having it. This moment presents subtle differences for the boy and the girl, being experienced by both in an intense and distressing way.

In the next phase, the latency phase, the child represses the sexual drive that was previously directed towards self. This libido is directed towards learning, towards social life. At this point, a defense mechanism, sublimation, occurs, which is the process in which all infantile sexual energy is diverted to other activities and plays a role in the development of the child, being the main characteristic of the latency period. Thus, the impulses experienced by the child would provoke unpleasant feelings (reactive impulses). In order to extinguish this displeasure, mental barriers of repression are built.

Freud (1905-1996) argues that during the latency period the psychic forces are built that will later prevent the course of the sexual drive, such as the mental barriers of shame and disgust.

These phases of child development are not satisfactorily completed, and when adolescence arrives, all the conflicting and distressing issues return with greater intensity, and not being able to bear this suffering, the individual slips into pathological symptoms.

The question of sexuality has been dealt with by Freud with proficiency and we will obtain in his research very important information.

Contrary to the thought that in childhood the sexual drive is absent, awakening only in puberty, Freud brings us valuable information about the development of sexuality from the first months of life of the baby, which allows us to evaluate the psychic states that involve the patient under analysis.

The question of infantile sexuality was a subject of controversy at the time it was raised by Freud in the Five Links of Psychoanalysis (1910[1909]), more specifically in the fourth Link. He shows that the main source of infantile pleasure is the excitation of certain, particularly excitable parts of the body: genitals, orifices of the mouth, anus and urethra, skin and other sensory surfaces. These places on the child's body, or erogenous zones, provide sexual pleasure. "The pleasure of sucking the finger, the enjoyment of sucking, is a good example of such autoerotic satisfaction from an erogenous zone". (Freud, 1909, p. 55).

In the "Three Essays on Sexuality" of 1905, Freud (1996) explains the relationship between infantile sexuality and the child's quest to understand the world around him. He states that the idea that the child has a sexual drive is ignored and that no literature mentions it. He adds that, in the first years of childhood, our memory is occupied by activities other than sexual drive and these are forgotten (amnesia) until the sixth or eighth year of l fe. He states that behind the infantile amnesia, there remain deep impressior s and traces, which have a decisive implication on the whole of the chilc's immediate development. He mentions that this amnesia allows the child to forget the beginning of his own sexual life.

For him, some professionals do not understand child sexuality, due to the confusion between sexual and genital and that the child's sexual activity is not directed to another but a satisfaction in his own body (self-erogenous).

In another wonderful work by Freud, "On the Sexua Theories of Children" (1906-1908), he says that the research carried out is from sources of observation of what children say and do, what adults remember from their childhood and report, and from deductions and conclusions from unconscious memories translated into the conscious.

In this text, he reports that adults do not pay enough attention to children's curiosity about their sexuality. In the years before puberty, every child is curious about sex, but unfortunately, adults shy away and confuse them with fanciful stories.

The experience lived by the child, in these phases of development, will influence the formation of his personality. In psychoanalysis, the personality is directly linked to the psychic apparatus, where we will have, in the first essay (first topic) of Freud, the division into: "Unconscious", "Pre-conscious" and "Conscious".

In his investigations of the cases he had the opportunity to analyze, Freud (1923-1996) found that there was something in the patients' minds, governing, controlling and repressing their psychic activity and that, in some cases, it offered a non-conscious resistance, because the patient did not perceive it, did not know what it was or how to describe it.

The psychic apparatus functions according to the law of the pleasure principle and the reality principle. When a representation, invested with affection with a portion of libido coming from the pulse, proves to be unbearable, capable of providing displeasure, then there is repression. But where does this repressed drive energy go?

We have then, within the psychic apparatus, where what has been repressed is, the Unconscious, which is governed by the pleasure principle, that is, which demands immediate satisfaction. As Mourano (2003,   p.25) asserts,   "our   psychic apparatus is governed by the pleasure principle.
dreams, failed acts, fantasies, symptoms and chistes are approached by psychoanalysis as formations of the unconscious".

The "Pre-conscious/Conscious" act together with the "Unconscious". The "Pre-conscious/Conscious" system is governed by the principle of reality, that which is within the perception of the subject and assimilated by him as real. In the "Pre-conscious" are the contents that can become conscious, because they are not under the force of censorship, they are latent contents. The "Conscious" are the perceptions of more immediate and certain character. Freud (1923) states that ideas or mental processes can be conscious for a brief period, it is transient, that is, what may be conscious now may not be later, but it can become conscious again under certain conditions.

The "Pre-conscious/Conscious" system also aims to achieve pleasure in a moderate way, contrary to the "Unconscious". It seeks to drain the energies linked to conscious representations slowly, as for example in study, where mental energy is discharged by this intellectual activity.

Thus, we have two systems: one, "Unconscious", which aims at absolute pleasure, which means the complete discharge of the drive tension; the other, "Pre-conscious/Conscious", which seeks moderate pleasure and thereby offers resistance to unconscious drives.

Freud realized that only the distinction between these systems was not sufficient to solve the many difficulties and obscurities in clinical analysis. Thus, he proposes three psychic instances: "ego" (mental/rational "I"), "superego" (ego ideal) and the "id" ("it"), thus comprising his second topic.

This differentiation is important, as has already been emphasized, since the unconscious becomes a quality present in each of the instances, and may be repressed or not. The "id" behaves as if it were unconscious, where the repressed contents are and is governed by the pleasure principle.

Freud (1923) explains that the "ego" seeks to apply rational influence to the "id", where the pleasure principle reigns, in order to replace it with the reality principle. It is the fight between what is perceptible, real and the instinct, the passions.

> While the ego is essentially the representative of the external world, of reality, the superego stands in contrast to it as the representative of the internal world, of the id. The conflicts between the ego and the ideal, as we are now prepared to discover, will ultimately reflect the contrast between what is real and what is psychic, between the external world and the internal world (FREUD, 1923-1996, p. 49).

Thus, we have: the "id" contains all the instincts and drives with which we are born, they are unconscious and do not take reality into account, the pleasure principle prevailing; the "ego" develops as the child gradually begins to perceive the outside world and seeks to adapt to it, and is the rational, organizing portion of the mind, containing the ability to plan and remember; and finally, we have the "superego" which develops as the child incorporates the rules dictated by parents and society, and may give rise to guilt.

Neuroses, which can erupt in the adult individual, are probably related to the pulsional conflicts provoked in some unsuccessful phase. Freud, with his studies and concepts, has greatly helped posterity to understand, analyze and help these individuals to work through these conflicts. In clinical practice, one observes the theories of psychoanalysis and, in many cases, one is surprised at how the patient's psychic suffering is linked to the phase of his previous life, when he was still a child.

Once again, the importance of these concepts stands out, because they will help to unravel the mind that is in suffering, providing the person who cries out for help, the hope of being able to find his balance and happiness.

4.2. THE CHILD IN THE VIEW OF BODY PSYCHOLOGY - CHARACTER BUILDING

There is no doubt about Sigmund Freud's precious contributions to the study of the mind and to the understanding of sexuality present in the development of the child from very early in life. However, for Body Psychology, the child is affected even in the gestational process. For this science, the energy fields of the parents are already taken into account at the moment when they wish to have their child. In this respect, the mother's womb is the first field where the child will develop, and a space where experiences of energetic movements occur at the cellular level. The moment of birth, the way the child comes into the world, is, for Body Psychology, primordial.

The development of the child, under the view of Body Psychology, according to Volpi and Volpi (2008), takes place in stages, ranging from gestation to puberty, where character formation occurs (which differs from Freudian ideas, because it considers development after the birth of the baby).

With regard to human development, aware of the Freudian questions about the sexuality of children, about the pulsional movements, Volpi and Volpi, in the beautiful book "Growing up is an Adventure" (2008), speak in a playful way about human development, dedicating a part of this work to the explanation of the stages of the emotional development of the child. They talk about the emotions involved, pleasant or unpleasant, experienced in the development of the little ones, since fertilization.

Thus, this process begins with the union of the ovum with the sperm. These are:

4.2.1. 1ª Development Stage - Sustainability

The first stage begins at fertilization. This is known as the period of sustenance. It is a crucial moment in human life and continues to decline after birth. It is at this time that the fetus has contact with its first environment, the mother's womb. This space must be welcoming, receptive and pulsating, in terms of energies, because everything that reaches the fetus through the umbilical cord, will be absorbed by it. At this time, there is much more than physiological needs happening, there are also major emotional and hormonal changes affecting the mother's body and mind, and she needs to be n balance, especially energetically, so that the baby continues to form. "It is important to know that the energy level of the embryo (low, normal or high) will be determined by the energy level of the mother's uterus (Reich-1987 in Volpi and Volpi, 2008).

This 1ª stage of development is subdivided into three phases: Segmentation, Embryonic and Fetal.

4.2.1.1.   Segmentation Phase

Through a link between the sperm and the ovum, life arises.

At this stage, a phenomenon called nidapo occurs, when the zygote, or young embryo, attaches itself to the wall of the uterus. From then on, cell divisions take place, for which there is a great consumption of energy at the cellular level.

According to Volpi and Volpi (2008), the mother's emotional changes affect mainly the energy field surrounding the being that is being formed. These changes can compromise the next phase, leading even to miscarriage.

4.2.1.2.   Embryonic Stage

This phase lasts until the tenth week of pregnancy. If all is well between the mother and the embryo, cell multiplications are taking place intensively, we can say "at full steam", so that the being grows and becomes a fetus.

This reminds me of an episode, referring to a case, which I called "Placenta Displacement", which occurred in my consultations with pregnant women. The mother, since she knew she was pregnant, felt very afraid. Still in this embryonic phase, she went through successive stresses at work and in her personal life. She did not feel prepared to be a mother and, what was worse, she did not receive support from her boyfriend. She said: "What am I going to do now?"; "It's not going to work out..."; "It's going to be difficult to work..."; "My boss is going to fire me..."; "I'm going to be huge...". In other words, this mother was, in fact, panicking.

This distressing moment was compromising embryonic development. Her gynecologist prescribed complete bed rest for a period of at least three months and recommended relaxation, as she had a very serious placental abruption. She came for psychotherapy sessions twice a week for two months, became aware of the seriousness, accepted being a mother and continued her life, becoming emotionally involved with the forming baby. She returned to work after three months of rest and stayed with the company until the eighth month of pregnancy. She remained in the therapeutic process, together with her partner, until the birth of the baby. The baby was welcomed with much love and joy in the family.

Volpi and Volpi (2008) explain that this is an energetic relapse and any type of stress or emotion at this time will contribute to preventing the embryo from attaching to the uterine wall. "A mother under emotional stress presents alterations in her internal secretions that go beyond the placental barrier producing changes in the psychophysiological balance of the child" (D'Andrea, 1994, p. 31).

4 .2.1.3.Fetal Stage

This phase begins at the end of the tenth week of pregnancy and gradually decreases until the first ten days after the birth of the child.

At this time, the development of the fetus' organs and maturational systems takes place. If everything went smoothly, with the minimum of stressful and distressing situations for the mother, the baby will be born in a situation of less energetic compromise in the constitution of his little body. If the opposite occurs, as almost happened in the case cited in the previous item, the baby will be the bearer of many damages in various organs and systems that were being formed at the time of the stress. Thus, "stress will form a cellular record that will be recorded as a signal, a mark and will be fundamental for the formation of the future characteristic traits of this new human being" (Volpi and Volpi, 2008, p. 133).

Navarro (2013) adds that, in embryonic life, stress situations affect genes. In fetal life, the mother's emogoes will resonate in the fetus, reflecting on the skin, hearing and circulatory system. In the newborn, stresses affect the five senses (touch, hearing, sight, smell and taste).

4.2.2. 2ª Development Stage - Incorporation

The second stage of development, also called the Incorporation Stage, begins shortly after birth and ends at the time of weaning, which is suggested to take place within nine months of the baby's life.

D'Andrea (1994) considers that birth is the greatest human experience, the first barrier to be realized in development, as well as the first separation of the many that the individual will have in life.

The main characteristic of this stage is that the baby leaves the womb to attach itself to the mother's breast. The baby, even in its immaturity, is able to regulate its needs by itself and will express this through crying, babbling and fussing. Volpi and Volpi (2008) recommend that it is necessary to prevent the baby from crying in a stressful way at this beginning of life, because the lacrimal glands are not yet fully developed, causing a dryness in the baby's eyes.

Spitz (1983) states that in this phase of human life, where the precarious maturation of the baby is perceived, the mother will be the facilitator for everything that the little one lacks.

We can understand at this point how necessary this relationship is for the emotional security of the child. It is a symbiotic contact, because they have been together for nine months, they have lived in deep emotions, so t is natural that this "stickiness" remains for a long time. In some cases, the mother finds it difficult to accept the help of the father, who is an extremely important figure for the healthy development of the child in this phase and in the following ones.

4.2.3. 3ª Development Stage - Produpao

The third stage, the Procreation Stage, begins with weaning and lasts until the end of the third year of life. It is at this time, separated from the mother, that the child begins to experience independence and autonomy, using all the physical and cognitive tools he has already acquired. Sphincter control is the hallmark of this stage. It is at this stage that children try to imitate adults in their search for identity. It is the awakening of a researcher. It is during this period that the little researcher tries to express curiosities, such as identifying names and relating them to objects. Their capacity for thought is heightened and their verbal expressions approach the language of adults.

4.2.4. Stage 4 of Development - Identification

The fourth stage of development and identification. It begins at the age of four. At this time, the child turns his attention to the discovery of the genitals. They also develop their ability to make identifications.

Their interests grow in relation to their bodies. The child is faced with the discovery of sexuality and explores the differences between boys and girls. The development of sexuality becomes stronger, she perceives herself as a sexual being. The first masturbations occur as a way of getting to know her body. The fantasies and prohibitions of adults at this time will only contribute to the formation of future neuroses. They do not understand that in the child's gestures there is no intention, that is, the way the child sees sexuality is different from an adult person.

In Reichian ideas, the expression of full sexuality would avoid the construction of somatic neuroses. "Sexuality is the center around which the life of society as a whole revolves and also the inner intellectual world of the individual" (Volpi, 2000, P.25).

According to Reich (1975), children, raised by adults contaminated by negative behavioral attitudes towards life and sex, contract a fear of pleasure, which leaves a physiologically supported sensation of fear of letting go. This craving, or fear of pleasure, is the basis on which neurosis is founded, the result of certain dictating and denying conceptions of life.

4.2.5. 5ª Stage of Development - Character Formation

The fifth stage, the Character Formation Stage, begins at the age of five and lasts until puberty. The process of identification becomes stronger with one of the representatives of the same sex; masturbation is more frequent and, with this, little by little, the child will find his own identity. If the child reaches this stage without frustration (5ª Stage), without repression, it will be able to reach the genital character. "The genital character is only a referential character, which means that we can have moments of genitality or genital rags, but we will hardly have a genital character" (Volpi and Volpi, 2008 p.140).

5. CHARACTER AND TRAITS

Many people confuse character with personality. Personality reflects the "I" of the subject, and is the result of the junction of physical aspects, temperament and character. While temperament is "the innate and particular disposition of each person, ready to react to environmental stimuli; it is genetically determined and concerns the person's mood" (Volpi and Volpi, 2008, p. 123), character "is the set of more elaborate behavioral forms determined by environmental, social and cultural influences, which the individual uses to adapt to the environment" (D'Andrea, 1994, p. 11).

It is important to remember that Reich was Freud's disciple and broke with psychoanalysis because it was not efficient in solving cases where the patient offered resistance. This resistance is not intentional, it is unconscious.

Reich extended Freudian ideas and elaborated the concept of character analysis, based on the patient's behavior. Reich (1995) says that the character can be understood as a solution to the sexual conflict of the child in the face of repressions of the environment in which it is inserted.

Volpi (2000) states that character can be understood as a defense, as a protective function of the ego, to avoid eminent suffering, and the sum total of what the ego shapes, that is, ways of acting and reacting characteristic of a unique personality.

Lowen (1977) states that the main point about character is that it represents a typical pattern of behavior or a habitual direction. It is a way of responding that is established, frozen or structured. It has a "characteristic" quality which always indicates a person's peculiar way of being (Lowen, 1977, p. 119).

Navarro (2013) comments that the formation of character is a consequence of modifications of the pulsional movements, felt by the baby in the environment. In other words, "character formation stems from the need of the living being to express or defend itself from certain situations that may intervene either from the inside, intrapsychic situation, or from the outside, interpsychic situation" (Navarro, 2013, p. 18).

Therefore, the character and the person itself is a result of the human understanding that was possible to be interpreted by the child at the specific moment, during and after the stages of development, what differentiates him from others, with attitudes and particular way of existence. "The development of a person's character depends on the degree of fixation or ccurapas on the various erogenous levels where most of the energy is concentrated" (Baker, 1980, p. 123).

In accordance with the above understanding, it is worth explaining that we are all influenced by various types of characters, however, the prevalence of one of them in the personality of the subject must be considered.

Thus, for body psychology, character formation depends not only on the fact that the drive and the frustration clash, but also on the way in which this occurred, including the developmental stage at which the conflicts formed, the sex of the person responsible for the frustration (anyone in the role of parent) and the contradictory conflicts in the frustrations themselves (Reich, 1995).

5.1. CONSIDERATIONS ON THE CHARACTER

In the formation of character, we must take into account the importance of the internal difficulties of each member of the family group, as a way of preventing future disorders.

> The final quality of the character - valid for both the typical and the particular - is determined by two factors: first, qualitatively, by the phases of libido development in which the process of character formation was most permanently influenced by internal conflicts, i.e., by the specific position of libido fixation. Thus, in qualitative terms, we can differentiate between depressive (oral), masochistic, genital-narcissistic (phallic) hysterical (genital-incestuous) and compulsive (anal-sadistic fixation) characters. Second, quantitatively, by the economy of libido, which depends on the qualitative factor. The former can also be labeled historical; the latter, the contemporary cause of the character form (REICH, 1998, p.171).

The influence of the child's caregiver on character formation must be taken into account, since repressive attitudes towards the freedom in which a child should develop contribute to the formation of neuroses which will affect the child's future life. "It is to the extent that a child experiences a sense of deprivation in the early years of life that genitality, independence and responsibility will be weakened" (LOWEN,1977, p.178).

The child in its essence is endowed with curiosity, spontaneity, joy, without rigidity, rich in hopes, motivating, reason for happiness for which it must be well guided, enriching it with love and providing the meaning to live fully.

In the following, some types of characters in Lowen's conception will be briefly explained and commented on, following the contributions of Reich and Baker.

5.2. SCHIZOID CHARACTER

Lowen (1982) points out that the schizoid character derives from schizophrenia, but is not a schizophrenic, although among them they have very similar tendencies in personality, such as the dissociation between thought and feelings. For him, the central issue of the schizoid personality is the lack of bodily pleasure in the relationship with his mother; this lack of pleasurable contact is felt as abandonment by the child who develops the feeling that no one cares for him. Rejection is the basic experience of the schizoid. "Rejection and hostility create fear in the patient that every search, every attempt at self-affirmation, will lead to this annihilation" (Lowen, 1982, p. 135).

For Lowen (1979), the schizoid, by ignoring or denying reality, expresses a mental confusion. This confusion denotes a schism, a lack of connection between the ego and the body, generating an absence of awareness of the sensations present in the body. Thus, the schizoid, having his contact with reality impaired, seeks in the illusion a resource of protection of the ego. Under this illusory perception, the individual becomes a prisoner, entering a vicious circle that demonstrates the inability to accept himself, finding in the dissociation between feelings and reality, a way to survive in the world.

For Reich (1998), schizophrenia has its origin in the organic, emotional and energetic imbalance. In a pregnancy, the mother not only maintains a nutritional relationship through the umbilical cord, but also an exchange of energies and emotions, which configures a bioenergetic coordination. In this way, it is explained that the rupture in this bioenergetic coordination that the little being undergoes, when in an indifferent and apathetic uterus, can generate schizophrenia. Thus, schizophrenia does not maintain a relationship with infantile experience (infantile development), as it happens in most psychic traumas of some patients, for example, neurosis. "It is this actual injury to the emotional structure, and not the remote infantile experience, which constitutes the dynamic factor of the illness" (Reich, 1998, p.409).

Therefore, the difference between the schizophrenic and the schizoid can be seen in the intensity of the perceptions of reality and the emotional value impregnated in the person. In the schizoid there are sensations of temporary loss of reality. In schizophrenia, because it involves a deeper emotional illness, there is a denial of reality (Lowen, 1979).

5.3. ORAL CHARACTER

The oral character has traces of early childhood in his personality, the strongest of which is dependence on others. They also often feel an inner emptiness. This behavior occurs because of the absence of gratification at this stage of development.

For Lowen (1977), in addition to the difficulty in dealing with reality, the oral character develops feelings of rejection, resentment and hostility. Their demands are for love. "The initial deprivation may be due to the actual loss of a warm and friendly mother figure, either through death, illness or absence determined by the need to work" (Lowen, 1982, p.138).

It is common to find in oral patients: an inability to be independent; a search for security and support; an urge to talk; impatience, restlessness, marked pessimism or melancholy; physical and mental fatigue; a morbid appetite for food; inclinations towards oral perversions; inner emptiness; difficulty in facing opposition, preferring to walk away rather than face an attack; an inability to cope with aggressive impulses.

In this type of character, the individual invests little or no energy in the realization of any task that requires a lot of effort, he can feel weakness and impotence in body movements, due to his breathing being superficial. Lowen (1982) states that due to the lack suffered by the individual, in the oral stage, the motor action is compromised, reducing the strength of the impulse to suck, that is, good breathing depends on the ability to suck air. Headache and profound fatigue are very common complaints. "Due to their low energy level, the oral person is subject to mood swings between depression and elation. The tendency to depression is pathognomonic of oral rags in the personality" (Lowen, 1982, p. 138).

Lowen (1979) explains that weakness in the arms and legs suggests an infantile defense; the voracious appetite can be interpreted as an attempt to supplement. Impatience and restlessness appear in response to unsatisfied desires, and he has difficulty in reaching out to the world, which leads to feelings of loneliness.

5.4. MASOCHISTIC CHARACTER

The masochistic character occurs because of a compromise in the anal stage. At this stage, we will also have a development of a psychopathic character, but with different reasons: in the psychopath, there is a denial of his feelings, the ego turns against his feelings, especially those of a sexual nature; the individual with a masochistic character is attached to suffering and lamentation, in reality, what the masochist complains about and, at the same time, what gives meaning to his life, he organizes himself within this logic. "[...] The masochistic character is not common, but the masochistic symptoms present in other neuroses are extremely frequent" (Baker, 1980, p. 153).

Reich (2009) says that the masochist presents a way of functioning turned to regrets. Their attitudes, originally directed to the objects, are also kept internally to the superego. That is, what the masochist understands of external reality, will be internalized, and it is possible to return this experience in the therapeutic process, in the transferential relationship between therapist and patient.

In this respect, Lowen (1977) states that the masochist's ego is crushed as if caught in a trap. He explains that there are two repressions in this perception: mentally, we will have a forced feeling; and genitally, the imposition of an obligatory toilet training. Therefore, the child feels the repression as an inward aggression, and so he internalizes the pressure before it, the aggression, merges into reality, mentally and physically.

Faced with such pressures, the child reacts strongly by crying, fighting or withdrawing. Through gaze, gesture and movement, he appeals to his mother for sympathy and understanding. This appeal to feeling is ignored, as it is considered that the mother knows more about life. "Energetic measures are employed: nagging, punishing, appealing to the child's love for the mother, and finally threatening to deprive the child of maternal love f he does not obey". (Lowen, 1977 p.195).

"The greatest damage that can be done to a child is contradiction between parents or inconsistency of their attitudes. Both cause the immobilization of the child and this is an essential factor in the evolution of the masochistic condition" (Baker, 1980, p.153).

The literature shows that the masochist and the oral suffer mainly from anxiety, in different ways, the masochist feels anxiety when he is under pressure from the professional environment or social relationships, while the oral, is anxious before facing the situation. It is common for patients with masochistic character to speak of feelings of being under pressure all the time. "The masochistic character does not complain of inner emptiness. On the contrary, he complains of feeling bursting, he complains of an inner pressure and of the inability to relieve the tension" (Lowen, 1977, p.194 and 195).

Thus, orality arises from deprivation at the beginning of the child's life and, in masochism, the suppression of the functions of independence occurs before the control of the physiological functions, naturally acquired in development, becomes conscious.

5.5. PSYCHOPATHIC CHARACTER

The psychopathic character comes from a blockage that occurs in the anal phase, and therefore fostered by emotional instability and sickened by seductive parents, which confuses the child in the search for independence and autonomy, natural in developmental experiences.

As mentioned earlier, in this character there is a predominance of denial of their feelings. "The denial of feelings is basically a denial of needs" (Lowen, 1982, p. 141). This denial is privileged by a strategy of making people dependent, so that they do not need to show their feelings and, in addition, they have a position of superiority which further satisfies their character. The denial of feelings contributes to hinder the therapeutic work, because it represents an egoic defense. Lowen (1982), when directing his gaze to the etiology of this structure, states that in the family, where there are seductive and authoritarian parents, they provide a rejection to the child. This rejection is based on the child's feeling of not being loved if he does not meet the adult's demands.

Seductive parents try to make their child submit to their demands, that is, they try to make their narcissistic needs satisfied by concealing the seduction. This game of seduction occurs when the seducer is of the opposite sex to the child. The aim is to make the child dependent on the affection of the seducing parent. He adds that from this relationship the child takes a challenging, competitive stance towards the same-sex parent, which will damage their identification with this parent, making the child identify more with the seducing mother or father.

The psychopathic personality also has a masochistic streak, resulting from

The important aspect of this structure, already in the adult individual, is his will to power and the need to dominate and control.

It is worth noting that the subjugation of the child by the seducing parent places the child within the power limits of the seducing parent, depriving the child of the right to be autonomous and independent.

5.6. RIGID CHARACTER

The basis of this structure is anchored in the fixation of the genital function, in the stage of identification, as a result of the Oedipal conflict.

At this stage, the child experiences and seeks erotic gratification. For them, erotic pleasure, sexuality and love are synonymous.

When they are reprimanded, usually when they are caught masturbating, i.e. when they express themselves lovingly and relaxedly in the face of harsh parental rejection, the child feels betrayed and attacked in his pride.

The rigid is always on the alert against situations or people who might take advantage of him. The distrust of being used and deceived is a very common behavior in this character. "The rigid individual is afraid of giving in, for he equates the act of submitting with losing oneself completely" (Lowen, 1982, p. 146).

Lowen used the term "rigid character" in bioenergetics to represent a factor common to several character types, such as the phallic-narcissistic, the hysterical and the narcissistic.

5.6.1. Falico-Narcissistic Character

According to Lowen (1977), the phallic-narcissistic character is a personality structure based on genitality. Although it can be found in women, its frequency is much higher in men. In this case, a striking feature of this character is related to the excessive value of his phallic image, whose ego invests in the seduction of women.

It is a moderate form of narcissism. Reich (2009) comments that this character (narcissistic phallic) exists to try to explain some characters that are difficult to name. It lies between compulsive and hysterical neuroses. "The compulsive is predominantly inhibited, reserved, depressive; the hysterical is nervous, agile, dominated by fear, eccentric" (Reich, 1998, p.209).

Lowen (1983) states that the concept of phallic-narcissism has two aspects. The first refers to the relationship between narcissism and sexuality, emphasizing erectile potency, with the phallus as a symbol. The second is related to a relatively healthy character, because narcissism is at a very small level.

For Baker (1980), the phallic-narcissistic character develops in the phallic phase (stage of identification, Volpi and Volpi, 2008), when the child perceives sexual differences, around 4 years of age. She presents a great suffering in relation to one of the parents, of the opposite sex to her, with the threat of castration. Her ego is usually strong in both sexes, as long as it guarantees satisfactory libidinal gratification.

5.6.2. Hysterical Character

The hysterical character is an ego structure anchored in the genital function, with fixation on the oedipal conflict, this conflict is based on the incestuous implications in the child's relationship with the opposite sex parent, causing a certain level of anxiety in the individual's sexual relationships in adulthood. "The Oedipus complex occurs when the child's natural attraction to the opposite-sex parent is blocked by the moralistic attitude of the child's same-sex parent" (Baker, 1980, p. 130). In this relationship, the child is affected by the anger he feels towards the opposite sex parent, the frustration of not realizing his desire, as well as the rejection the father has shown. This makes the child feel repressed. "The damage done to the hysterical character is the rejection of her love on the genital plane" (Lowen, 1977, p. 241).

Baker (1980) states that the hysterical character presents a constant desire for genital contact, following with the desire to escape, that is, they firt openly or disguised, performing seductive games, through looks, the way of speaking and walking, very provocative, but when the act is about to be realized, they change their posture and can escape or become passive. He adds that the person with this character structure does not achieve full sexual satisfaction, because there is no complete discharge of energy, causing a numbness, increasing their anxiety and becoming a lifeless, restless and volatile organism.

5.6.3. Narcissistic Character

Lowen (1983) says that narcissism is a pathological condition. In this case, the subject invests in his own image, to the detriment of the self, that is, he denies his feelings, there is a dissociation between the ego and the body.

The emotions of sadness and fear, being expressions of human vulnerability, are repressed in this individual, because he needs to pass the image of being strong, of having power.

He argues that the ego of this character is too grandiose, which gives them a connotation of always being the best among other people. "Narcissistic characters are completely out of touch with the world of feeling and are ignorant of how they should relate to other people in a real and human way" (Lowen, 1983, p.26).

He adds that during the period in which the child discovers his sexuality, during the period of identification, he was exposed to great humiliation, added to the seductions of his parent. This seduction aims to make the child see himself as something very special, in order to make him feel superior. "After being rejected and humiliated, the child is more easily seduced into serving the parent" (Lowen, 1983, p. 98).

Lowen (1983) also states that narcissistic characters can be cruel, exploitative, sadistic or destructive towards another person because they are insensitive to the suffering or feelings of others. The quest for power is a way of protecting oneself against humiliation and overcoming a feeling of inferiority.

5.7. GENITAL CHARACTER

For Reich (2009), the genital character has a balance between tension and satisfaction of libido. He explains that the ego of the individual with this character also has courapas, however, he has the capacity to control them, which makes them flexible. Therefore, this malleability contributes to increase their ability to give themselves to the other, which is configured, great possibilities of surrender to love. "The genital character can be cheerful, but angry when necessary. It reacts to the loss of the object with sadness, but is not overwhelmed by it. It can love intensely and enthusiastically and hate passionately" (Reich, 2009, p. 175).

> A genital character is one whose individual meets the requirements of health. That is to say: the person is well enough integrated and emotionally free enough to be able to express himself sufficiently and to know how to satisfy himself in terms of his life. Since he has satisfactions at his disposal, he does not accumulate tensions or develop chronic armpits. Ideal health is, of course, only a concept, not something that flows and allows a wide range of manifestations" (Baker, 1980, p 125).

In this way, we can consider the individual with a genital character structure capable of living in balance, without fear of frustration. He gives himself to love in its pure and innocent form, because love has an admirable power to provide happiness, stimulating the other feelings to conquer his freedom. When you love, you are healthy, you break the armor and the rings that surround the body, which can move, producing life and inner renewal. For this, it is necessary that the child is welcomed with respect by their parents, without projecting their longings and unfulfilled desires, because what they expect is to live with freedom and grow according to their own natures and for this, they expect their parents to be present to help them.

We should not forget, however, that the therapeutic process seeks to treat people and not types of character. We try to focus on the patient, on his energetic condition, on his interaction with his body, on his relationship with people and on his way of seeing and accepting life.

6. ORGONE ENERGY - CHARACTERISTIC TRAITS OR COVERAGE - BODY SEGMENT OR ARMOR SEGMENT

In clinical experience, we have found it very difficult to separate the basic character of a patient from the characteristic traits.

These characteristic traits are directly linked to the character, they have all the characteristics of the character, but they only serve as a cover for protection, defense of psychic conflicts, which occur in the dimension between internal and external reality, originated during the development process and which served as the elaboration of the basic character.

All this is related to the body segments, or couragas segment, defined by Reich, which in turn is linked to the energy flowing in and out of the organism.

6.1. ORGONE ENERGY

Body Psychology considers the energy that circulates in our body as fundamental in the process of analysis and treatment of the patient. This vital energy is called orgone, it circulates inside and outside the body. "Orgone energy is a completely new form of energy, fundamentally different from electricity and magnetism" (Reich, 2009, p.114).

In practical cases, it is verified that patients who present blockages in the flow of this energy, have a better discernment when these blockages are relaxed or loosened. With this, the psychotherapeutic treatment flows satisfactorily, leading this patient to have a better perception of his body and, consequently, to a more balanced quality of life.

> In encouraged human organisms, the orgone energy is bound up in the chronic concentration of the muscles. The body orgone only starts to flow freely as soon as the armor ring is loosened. The first reaction is clonic tremors, together with the sensation of itching or tingling. Clinically, this reaction means that the cuff is giving way and the body orgone is being released (REICH, 1998, p.344).

The energies of the body in dissonance, the tormented ego and the deficient body clash and produce the disharmony of the personality. Conflicts manifest in the consciousness and complexes take shape, aggravating feelings with insecurity, fear, isolationism, abandonment of love and absence of self and other people.

Therefore, vital energy commands our external responses based on internal experiences. Following this reasoning, Damasio adds that, "the body provides a fundamental reference for the mind" (Damasio, 1998, p. 254).

6.2. BODY SEGMENTS OR ARMOR SEGMENTS

Body psychology reveals the existence of segments in the body, arising from the development process. In these segments, energetic blockages can occur as a form of defense of the organism. These blockages are called courages.

Reich (1995) states that courages are a form of ego defense against physiological (internal) manifestations and social (external) issues, wh ch leads to chronic mental and bodily stiffening of the ego, affecting the individual's total personality.

According to Reich (1995), the formation of energy congestion in the body is arranged in seven segments or rings, which he called segments or rings of courages, they are: "ocular", "oral", "cervical", "thoracic", "diaphragmatic", "abdominal" and "pelvic".

Navarro (2013) explains that the idea of "muscular character armor", for Reich, presents itself as a defense for intrapsychic and interpsychic conflicts, where it is understood that it is in the internal (intrapsychic) and external (interpsychic) perceptions that the "armor" is formed so that the subject can balance in life. "When internal or external dangers threaten the psychic balance of a person, repeatedly damaging the instinct of conservation, then the defensive structure, the armor, the armor is formed" (Navarro, 2013a, p. 19).

Navarro (2013b) clearly describes each of these segments, placing them in levels, as shown below:

f) The first level ("ocular" segment) comprises the seat of three senses: sight, hearing and smell. He says that these senses must be integrated, i.e. function together as soon as the baby is born, otherwise they will lead to a confused and distorted understanding of reality by the individual;

g) At the second level ("oral" segment), we have the mouth that enables the child to appropriate the environment through the function of taste and to introject or reject this environment through breastfeeding. He adds that it is through this cavity that we feed and perceive reality, from birth, in terms of pleasure, displeasure, frustration and rejection. It clarifies that a malfunction, with dissatisfaction in these first two levels, can lead the adult individual to return to a phase of childhood, thus presenting an infantile behavior;

h) In the third level ("cervical" segment) and the fourth level ("thoracic" segment), composed of the neck and the upper thorax, we find the primary narcissism, necessary for our survival. He states that when a moralistic education prevails, it leads to secondary narcissism, which represents a sick personality.

> The repression of primary narcissism only exacerbates the narcissistic drive, which then turns into secondary narcissism: the upper part of the thorax is swollen, in this case with hatred, suffocating all affective potentiality and compressing, both literally and figuratively, the heart (NAVARRO, 2013a, p. 65).

It also states that under the influence of secondary narcissism, the individual has a stagnation of energy in the neck which leads to rigidity of the neck.

neck to the spine, compromising the mobility of the neck.

He explains that the origin of his conflict arises from the fear of feeling his narcissism hurt by some disappointment, involving separation, rejection, abandonment and loneliness;

i) The fifth level ("diaphragmatic" segment), compromises the diaphragm muscle that is related to the survival of the being, because it is responsible for the metabolism of tissues, such as: absorbing oxygen (O_2) and eliminating carbon dioxide (CO_2) through respiration. Without this process, energy distribution is impaired. The emotional charge manifested in this region is anxiety. It cuts off the breath when waiting for something much desired, generating expectation by a fear that comes from the first level to the diaphragm. If the opposite occurs, if the energy of the diaphragm is dammed, there will be a return of energy that should circulate to the pelvis to the upper body, causing agitations, somatizations, among them, the manifestations of gastrointestinal disorders, headaches, gastritis, gastric ulcer, etc.. The individual, in this state, presents an emotional conflict, based on guilt and anxiety;

j) The sixth level ("abdominal" segment) contains the muscles of the abdomen (obliques, rectus and transversus), the muscles of the back and sides of the trunk. At this level, we realize the functional relationship with the mouth and the diaphragm.

k) The seventh level ("pelvic" segment), which is represented by the pelvis, contains the muscles of the pelvis and the lower limbs. The blockage here is always secondary, because the blockages have already started from the first segment. This blockage occurs because of a moralistic education, a pelvic rigidity occurs, as an unconscious denial of a full genital sexuality. He states that the individual has little or almost no pelvic sensitivity, describing the sensations as dead or empty.

The relationship between these levels of blockages, according to Navarro (2013), can occur very frequently, that is, dynamically, because, depending on the somatization, one level may reflect on another.

Thus, the first level, which represents the eyes, ears and nose, can be connected to the second level (mouth). The mouth can be considered as a door through which fear can enter and thus provoke the anxiety of terror. This generates anguish which can be reflected in the fifth level (diaphragm).

The second level (mouth) is linked to the seventh level (pelvic) due to genitality and excretion.

The third level (neck), according to him, is the seat of self-control and also where the defenses of the instinct of conservation are located. This level can be linked to the fourth (thoracic), the fifth (diaphragmatic) and the seventh (pelvic) levels, due to narcissism, which is based in the neck, causing the individual to control his anxiety and make painful efforts to achieve his goals. The link with the seventh (pelvic) level demonstrates his inability to surrender.

The fourth level (thoracic) is a passage zone between the first three levels and the next three.

The fifth level (diaphragmatic) is considered to be the most important, as one cannot live without breathing; it functions as a distributor of energies and is connected to the other levels.

The sixth level (abdomen) is a bridge between the diaphragm (fifth level) and the pelvis (seventh level). The latter depends on the others to function properly.

It is convenient to deal here with sexual stasis, linked to the seventh level (pelvic). In the understanding of Baker (1980), stasis is installed when full genital release is not possible, causing a strong tension and causing a muscular stiffening (courapa), specifically, in the lateral walls of the abdomen (sixth level), by a tensioning of the spinal and pelvic muscles. These tensions appear in the individual's behavior, when he becomes irritable or moody, which will contribute to irrational attitudes in interpersonal and intrapersonal relationships.

In relation to sexual stasis, Reich (2009) explains that the function of orgasm is the key to the problematics of neurosis. That is, the repression of sexual energy affects the energetic harmony of the organism. Thus, "the elimination of sexual stasis through biological orgasmic discharge removes all kinds of neurotic manifestations. And the difficulty to be overcome is largely of a social nature" (Reich, 2009. p. 03). "The psychosomatic structure is the result of a clash between social and biological functions. The function of orgasm is the measure of psychophysical functioning, because it is in it that the function of biological energy is expressed" (Reich, 1975, p. 320).

> If the stasis is not corrected, it can continue to spread, causing a regression to pregenital levels and the development of a neurotic condition. Dammed energy floods the organism, reactivating the pregenital erogenous zones which seek a way to discharge it. This gives rise to the reproduction of

infantile fantasies and the revival of the Oedipal problem, which only reinforces the defense mechanisms. Trapped in a vicious circle, the organism has no way out until the energy overflows in the form of symptoms (BAKER, 1980, p. 128).

Thus, repression in the developmental stages of the child will contribute to the retention of energy at any level and this is related to the courapa segments present in the adult body.

The simple fact of the awareness of experiencing pleasure without guilt, helps the patient to love the body, to move the muscles, reducing physical tensions, derived from conflicts of an emotional nature. Thus, the individual gradually expands his perception, allowing himself to live and to seek new realizations.

6.3. CHARACTER TRAITS OR COVERAGE

Character rags or covering, as we have previously stated, are character rags that the individual assumes as a form of defense, to organize himself and be accepted in the world.

Navarro (2013) explains that, in the face of inadequate demands on biophysiological development, it will cause marked sensations of emotional dissatisfaction in the child that present themselves in their behavior and, therefore, the character may present itself as a cover for these experiences of frustrations. In this way, in the face of alterations in neuromuscular functioning, resulting from blockages in body segments, they will stimulate the construction of character and, later, of character.

Thus, the characterization will be a hedge, because it covers moments that were not possible to elaborate when the emoption occurred, arising from unsatisfied psychological elements.

Navarro (2013) defines characteriality as a set of characteristic rags that shape the so-called normality of today's neurotic man.

This can be exemplified when we come across a patient with a schizoid character, with a hysterical overlay. During the analysis, we try to collect the patient's history and, with the application of some techniques, we arrive at the diagnosis. In this example, we will notice the prevalence of the schizoid character and that, in order to protect himself from distressing situations that offer danger to his ego, the patient creates this hysterical cover. This neurotic cover originates from Oedipal conflicts.

It should be clarified that this hysterical cover is part of the individual's behavior and should not be removed immediately, as it would expose his fragile self. What happens in practice, in therapy, is to manage this cover, so that the patient can mature, making the cover less rigid, which will result in a better understanding of himself, presenting more expressiveness in his acts and attitudes.

In clinical practice, it has been observed that the more rigid the personality of the individual, he may present more than one cover, i.e. more than one character trait.

It should be made clear that it is not a question of labeling the patient, but of demonstrating the importance of identifying the character and the characteristic traits in order to develop a therapeutic project that will help him/her to better organize his/her life.

Navarro (2013) explains that compulsive character cover (phallic-anal and hystero-anal) can be seen in borderline character, understood here as temperamental-character, with cover of mild intensity and with the intention of preventing the explosion of a repressed psychotic core. For him, the oral character is the borderline character. He considers that we have oral traits in any type of character.

Thus, in the borderline character, with compulsive covering, the child will present a rigid behavior, which makes it uncreative and linked to a schematized routine, that is, in the face of changes in the day to day will provoke anguish. This rigidity may be the result of a severe education in the control of sphincters during the child's anal phase.

A very common example, reported by a patient who had masochistic rags, occurred in his childhood, and when he made outings with his parents, whether at the mall or supermarket, it usually happened with his mother, and he felt like going to the bathroom. He manifested himself repeatedly, without being answered in his desires. Usually, he would receive the following answers: "This is not the place for that..."; "Wait until you get home..."; or worse, "I'll take you there...", and he would not leave the place. He did not have many options, either he did it there, in his clothes, because he could not stand the physiological pressure and faced the discomfort and humiliation, or he tried to repress himself. It was noticeable at the time he was telling his story that he was contracting his legs and putting his hand on his stomach, showing real discomfort, as if he was feeling the same sensations as before. This shows the reflection of distress in his body.

There are also reports of children growing up in the care of strict adults who demand that they use the toilet without being emotionally and physiologically prepared to do so.

Navarro (2013) comments on the repressive education and the pleasures of adults to "control" the child. The child understands that he must eliminate his feces not when his body wants, but when his parents allow it. He also explains that the emotional manifestations (constipation, chronic diarrhea, etc.) are installed as a defense of the individual, resulting from complications present in the psycho-affective development of the child. With regard to diarrhea, it is understood as an expression of strong anguish, caused by feelings of being demanded beyond what it can bear. In the case of constipation, the cause would be feelings of having to hold it in and is also related to anxiety about sphincter education. "Psycho-pedagogical prevention consists of giving a lot and expecting little from the child throughout the anal period, so that he or she will gradually learn to manage bowel movements without giving exaggerated value to feces" (Navarro, 2013a, p. 119).

It is worth remembering that we have rags of various kinds of characters and that we should not hold ourselves to a rigid idea such as: "My character is oral, the world is over"!

In the case of depression, there is a prevalence of this character by fixation in the oral phase, however, there are in these individuals, rags of other characteristic types. "[...] We can find rags and oral tendencies in almost all individuals who present themselves for analytic therapy" (LOWEN, 1977, p. 153).

7. STRESS - DEPRESSION

Nowadays, more than ever, there is a growing inability to overcome the difficulties imposed by life. The ability to maintain stability in the most varied situations and opportunities is related to psychological maturation, conducive to the acquisition of values relevant to a harmonious existence.

As we have seen so far, the psychological being is forged by the experiences suffered in the different stages of his psycho-affective development, which will determine his maturation, understood here as the individual's ability to discern and maintain his "self" in balance.

We do not want to say that the cause of all the ills that afflict man today is based on the phases in which he felt constrained to repress his impulses, due to a distorted culture, sedimented in prejudice, pride, lack of affection, etc.

Today's modern life, which generates stress and anguish, also contributes greatly to triggering the mechanism of anxiety and various phobias, which wears out the psychological core with regrettable dysfunctions in the physical body.

However, we cannot deny that a psychologically stable individual will cope better with these difficulties, not letting himself be affected by events, than one in which there is fragility in his psychological structure, as happens with depressive individuals.

The depressive state, as we shall see later, is very much related to character formation. But we should also deal with stress, because, as will be shown, it can contribute to the onset of depression.

7.1. STRESS

For Margis et al (2018) the stress process is defined as a state constructed by the perception of stimuli that increase and trigger an emotional response, which contributes to disturbing the homeostatic balance, which leads to brain processes by increasing adrenergic secretions, producing systemic manifestations with physiological and also psychological disorders.

They conclude that various stressful situations occur over the years and the responses to them vary greatly among people in their form of presentation, and that various psychopathologies may appear with unspecific symptoms of depression or anxiety, or defined psychiatric disorders.

> At many times in life a person may experience difficult situations and such intense suffering that they think something is going to break inside them, that they will not be able to stand it, that they will lose control over themselves... that they will go mad. This can occur when one loses someone very close and dear, in highly stressful situations, in which the individual finds himself with many doubts and does not realize the possibility of asking for help and / or solve alone such situation. (BOCK, 2002, p. 346).

In view of this, the commitment to reality, the difficulties of emotional expressions, can be perceived in individuals with complaints of suffering, no matter if it is due to panic, death of a loved one, some type of phobias, Obsessive Compulsive Disorder (OCD) or another situation that involves an energetic depletion of the organism. All of us at some point have gone through similar situations.

The difference lies in the way we understand and learn to deal with, transform or sublimate the situations that present themselves. And when it is not possible to sublimate, we only repress, store in the unconscious, and this content may be returning in the face of a stimulus that refers us to the initial trauma, in this case, without intervention, it appears in the form of symptoms and the individual has difficulty organizing, understanding what is happening.

Selye (1978) puts it that stress is essentially the rate at which the body wears out. Anyone who finds themselves, either on their own or through others, in a debilitating or stressful situation has a vague idea of what stress represents. Feelings of fatigue, anxiety or malaise are subjective sensations of stress. In any situation, weariness is just a result of all these; hence the current definition of stress as an unspecific bodily response to any form of demand.

With regard to research on stress, the author comments that it had been very hampered because it did not have objective and measurable indices to evaluate it precisely, until, about forty years ago, it was discovered that stress was the cause of certain changes in the structure and chemical composition of the body, and these could be evaluated accurately. Some of these changes are merely signs of damage; others are manifestations of the body's adaptive reactions, its defense mechanism against stress. The totality of these changes - the stress syndrome - is called the General Adaptation Syndrome (GAS).

Selye (1978) divided S.A.G. into three phases:

a) Alert phase - this phase begins with the contact of the individual with the stressor. The person cannot maintain the balance of his body and may present the following symptoms: stomach pain, tension and pain in the muscles, diarrhea, among others;

b) Resistance phase - in this phase the person tries to react and return to normality. Your body may or may not respond to this effort.

c) Exhaustion Phase - is a critical phase, basically there is a return to the Alert Phase, the person can succumb to the stressful stimulus and lead to death.

The nervous system and the endocrine (or hormonal) system play important roles in maintaining resilience during stress. They help maintain the structure and functionality of the body, making it stable despite exposure to stress or stressors such as nervous tension or infection. This stability, acting in defense of the body, is called homeostasis.

Navarro (2013) speaks of the importance of the functioning of the living being in maintaining balance to ensure homeostasis. He points out that we are endowed with an energetic charge that pulsates in a circular way, animating the body and interacting with the environment, in order to form a cosmic energetic pulse.

The individual weakened in his psychic structure, under stress, may, in a certain way, evolve into a depression, because he feels that his suffering is too unbearable, surrendering to discouragement, nostalgia and self-deprecation. In this case, the stress may act as a trigger, a stimulus, bringing out from his unconscious the traumas suffered in his development process, where there was a fixation on the stage in which he suffered repression.

7.2. DEPRESSION

According to the World Health Organization - WHO (2018), depressive disorder is common worldwide. It is estimated that more than 300 million people suffer from it. These people may experience symptoms of mood fluctuations and difficulty with short-lived emotional responses to the challenges of everyday life. Depression can be considered a critical health condition, considering the duration and intensity that is experienced by the affected individual.

Thus, depression can cause a great deal of internal suffering and can keep the person away from work, school and family activities.

In the clinical picture, the depressed person shows no interest in things and situations that used to be a source of satisfaction and joy. We can say that he brings with him conditions that hinder the movements of reactions in life, as if he lacked strength, stimuli for simple accomplishments, such as feeding and taking care of his own body. It is perceived that the meaning of life is altered.

The individual with a balanced psychic structure, that is, healthy, can feel good, even having moments of sadness and anxiety, since these issues are part of the life of all of us. Thus, he or she directs the emotions in an organized way, facing the obstacles that are presented to him or her, and that are part of the process in which he or she is immersed, which will strengthen him or her and allow him or her to develop the capacity for growth and to store knowledge.

For Winnicott (2013), people with depression have a sense of guilt and, in more severe cases, distrust and delusions of persecution. The depressive would be full of deep guilt, as if he were internally wounded, preventing them from leading their lives with enthusiasm and creativity. He adds that depression is very complex, citing some types, such as: "[...] chronic depression, with more or less paranoid anxiety; reactive depression, associated with mourning; and severe melancholia" (Winnicott, 2013, p. 87).

A distinction should be made between depression and melancholy. In clinical practice, melancholy appears in the discourse of patients as a feeling of deep sadness, an inner emptiness, accompanied by a desire to cease to exist, and they speak of various forms of suicide attempts. Although depressed individuals also suffer from sadness, feelings of loss and lack of energy, there is no desire for death in their discourse.

Freud, in Draft G (1996), says that in melancholia there is a desire to recover something lost, which is configured in a mourning. "Melancholia consists in mourning for loss of libido" (Freud, 1996, p.247).

It is considered that the desire or the will to live in the melancholic becomes fragile, almost nonexistent. According to Navarro (1996), the tendency to melancholy can be installed very early in the life of the individual, occurring in the first 10 days after birth, due to the difficulty of the baby to organize in this new space. "The neonatal period, the symbiotic period, is the period of breastfeeding and weaning, characteristic of motherhood, a period of intense and deep affective resonance" (Navarro, 1996, p.44).

In depression, according to Del Porto (2018), not all depressed individuals present the symptoms considered typical, for example: faced with a feeling of emptiness, not all patients report the subjective feeling of sadness; others speak mainly of the loss of the ability to take pleasure in activities, in general, decreasing interest in what happens around them; they feel fatigued, with lack of concentration and a great loss of energy.

Fenichel (1966) comes to clarify about this subject, that the individual is trapped in a state in which his self-esteem is affected by guilt, leading him to return to a pre-genital posture, due to having his vital needs deficient and for presenting lack of not having been met in his desires. And if their narcissistic needs are not satisfied, their self-esteem will fall to a dangerous point, thus configuring itself: on the one hand, the pre-genital fixation of these people is manifested by a tendency to react to frustrations with violence, with oral dependence; on the other, with impulses to try to get what they need through propitiation and submission. "The conflict between these two contradictory forms of behavior is characteristic of persons who exhibit this predisposition" (Fenichel, 1966, p. 436).

According to "The Diagnostic and Statistical Manual of Mental Disorders" - DSM-5 (2014), the person with depression presents feelings of emptiness, sadness, accompanied by psychosomatic alteration that affect the functional capacity of the individual.

The background of depression is a decline in vital energy within the body, i.e. due to conflicts in the perception of oneself, the individual does not believe that he or she is capable of reacting to the difficulties that arise in life, i.e. they are deeply discouraged. Their phrases in these severe cases of depression are almost always: "I have no interest in anything..."; "I feel tired, I don't want to do anything...". Therefore, a disorganized mind and an emotionally affected body lead to conditions of disharmonies at the level of organic tissues and, consequently, illness is embodied in the body.

> [...] Depression is not a struggle, but a decrease in energetic processes and the formation of impulses. Energy does not seek to discharge itself; this is a genital function. On the contrary, it goes up to the head, seeking contact with the world. Given the severe blockage in the path of the energetic flow to the arms, it follows the infantile path leading to the head and mouth. This is what produces the volubility of the oral character during the period of elation [...] in elation, the oral character reverts to an infantile stage. It is the seeking of the breast with the mouth. In this stage, there is no need to be independent; the baby can rely on the strong arms of the mother to support him. (LOWEN, 1977, p. 168 - 169).

Depression is directly linked to the question of orality. In the process of character formation, the subject maintains a fixation on the oral stage, thus presenting an oral or borderline character. "A diagnosis of the presence of orality would be justified on the basis of a history of repeated depressions" (Lowen, 1977, p. 157).

Body Psychology clarifies that, this fixation on the oral stage, leads us to consider a deep and deficit dissatisfaction, at the moment of child development, where the child should be involved with feelings of love and have his physiological needs satisfied.

Lowen (1983) corroborates this assertion by stating that depressed people have an affective lack that comes from unsatisfied oral needs, arising from the deprivation of maternal love, from the warmth that this love could provide, compromising the exchange of good energetic emanations between them, which will contribute to the formation of the oral character. If the effect of this lack is not so intense, the individual may show oral traits in his personality.

Navarro (2013) reveals that feeding is a crucial moment in the child's life. When the relationship between mother and baby is satisfactory, the newborn when eating, feels loved, welcomed, nestled, with deep feelings of calm, leading to well-being. The opposite will cause dissatisfaction, leading to depressive and aggressive behavior. He also adds that this depressiveness accompanies a decrease in sexual desire in adulthood, resulting from poor breastfeeding, abrupt or early weaning.

We have seen so far that depression has a psycho-affective background that involves an energetic stasis at a certain early stage of the child's life, culminating in the predisposition to depress. In many situations that arise in our lives, with a pathological level of stress, the individual feeling weakened or pressured, can refer to these poorly elaborated childhood experiences.

The depressed individual loses humor and love for himself. For this reason, it is essential to break the psychological shackles responsible for the contempt of oneself, for the shrinking and self-denial so that he can have a clear vision of reality and the means to live it well, directing him to the conquest of fullness.

Thus, the help of health professionals (doctor, psychiatrist, psychologist, etc.) is important for the subject to strive to overcome depressive feelings, so that self-worth is part of his inner growth scheme, which will enable him to achieve his recovery.

8. DEPRESSION AND BODY PSYCHOLOGY

Body psychology can be of great help in the treatment of depression. Not only by its precepts (vegetotherapy and bioenergetic analysis), which brings a substantial clarification about its causes, but also by the various techniques that can be employed, favoring the loosening of energetic blockages and making the patient have a new perception of his body, enabling the restoration of a healthier life.

Of the many techniques used, we can mention the "actings", developed by Federico Navarro and the breathing technique, disseminated by Lowen. In the application of the "actings" techniques, as Navarro prescribes, the unblocking should be carried out from the first level and gradually continue to the others.

In clinical practice, I use vegetotherapy (methodology developed by Navarro) a lot and have received good results with my patients. Vegetotherapy restores the neurovegetative function that has been altered by oral repression. In the treatment a very simple technique is proposed, with the application of four "actings" of the mouth: open mouth, sucking, chewing and showing the teeth. The results have been surprising, because we can prove the theory in practice.

8.1. BODY PSYCHOLOGY IN THE CLINIC

In clinical experience, it is noticeable that getting sick involves changes in the perception of love. Whether in the way we were loved, or how we love the other, the object of our affection.

Reich (1975) explains that psychic health depends on orgasmic potency, that is, on the individual's capacity to give himself to life and love. He considers that psychic illnesses are the result of a disturbance of the natural capacity to love. In analysis, the restoration of this potency is sought.

The person who comes for psychotherapeutic treatment is suffering in some way. Their complaints are usually related to anxiety, depression, confusion, frustration or being unhappy with their life. Her expectations at this time are that therapy will enable her to improve these conditions, to change her way of functioning in the world, perhaps even to have some joy. This suffering means that, at some point in her life, she has been hurt. Lowen (1997) says that some patients are aware that their childhood was unhappy, that they felt frightened and alone, but most believe that their unhappiness is the result of some weakness or flaw in their personality.

The psychotherapeutic treatment, by Body Psychology, involves understanding the patient's history in a broad context that goes beyond the symptoms presented by him, because we consider that the body actively participates in this process.

In psychotherapy, which is timeless, we seek to loosen the armor, not to remove it, but to provide integrative functionality between body, mind and energy.

By starting the analysis of the character, a psychic operation, which proceeds according to a defined plan and developed from the peculiar structure of the patient, one reaches the depths of the unconscious, which makes it possible to go beyond the understanding of spoken language, the verbal method used by Psychoanalysis (Volpi and Volpi, 2008).

When the patient becomes aware of the physical and psychological tensions, there are noticeable changes in the body and its behavor. Coulrages are not removed because they exist as a precaution of the egc to avoid greater suffering. The aim is to reduce the rigidity of the armor in order to increase cognitive flexibility, widen the visual field and thus increase the spontaneous capacity of the individual, with the maturation of his psychological core.

Thus, in the face of stresses, situations that require changes in behavior and attitudes, it will be less difficult to organize. Lowen (1977) explains that, for the acquisition of pleasure in life, it is necessary that the maturation of the ego occurs. And this happens through the perception of bodily sensations and the expression of feelings. An integration into the total personality takes place, i.e. energy, mind and body are organized.

The main objective is to rescue the energy trapped in vital points of the body: eyes, mouth, neck, diaphragm, abdomen, stomach and pelvis. In this process, the work of breathing and unblocking the first three segments is done. Although they are people with the same diagnosis, it is understood that each one feels and expresses themselves in a unique way. Therefore, the treatment is always thought and focused on the basic character and the characteristic traits of that person.

The issue of breathing is one of the main focuses of Body Psychology, because it is in breathing that we mobilize our most primitive feelings, besides mobilizing more energy and reducing tension.

> Inadequate breathing causes anxiety, irritability and tension. It underlies a number of symptoms such as claustrophobia and agoraphobia. The claustrophobe feels as if they cannot breathe in a closed place. The agoraphobe feels afraid of open places because they stimulate his breathing. Any difficulty in breathing causes anxiety. If the difficulty is severe it can lead to panic or terror (LOWEN, 1984, p.33).

It is of utmost importance to be mindful of the patient's timing, while making use of all movements and techniques during the session,

Great care should be taken when working with breathing in the therapeutic setting, due to the latent content that can emerge without prior knowledge of the patient's history, because without this care, the work may not have a beneficial effect, or have an opposite effect to that expected.

In most cases, the patient is not aware of these tensions and may not be prepared to deal with all the issues surrounding the patient's condition.

blockage of breathing. This care is justified because, in the first relationships of life, some people may experience great suffering and, as a defense and protection, there may be a blockage of the diaphragm, the passage of energy is altered, diminished, and the consequences are the alteration of organic vitality, compromising the health of the body and opening paths to psychopathologies.

It is common for patients to complain of a lack of energy when they have this blockage. They usually say: "I'm very tired, I have no energy, but I can't explain why...". Even when this is the case, it is not always possible to start working more intensively with breathing. It is basically the ability to feel the other person that triggers the "alert". This "alert" is only possible when we maintain a connection with the patient, what Body Psychology calls a "Radiant Bridge". In this process, an energetic field occurs between therapist and patient, which will facilitate the therapeutic process.

In this way, when we breathe deeply, we come into contact with deeper feelings, in old, primary emotions, and this will certainly cause fear, anguish of all kinds, so we reduce the field of breathing. Lowen (1986) explains that by inhibiting breathing, we prevent the release of feeling and, consequently, the suppression of feelings leads to inhibition of the breathing process.

She was once approached by a 38-year-old single man, a physical education teacher. He said he had to take time off work because his sister, with whom he had lived since he was 12, had died of a massive heart attack two months ago. He said that the pain was too great. According to his account, he had suffered successive frustrations in his personal and professional life. He commented that he felt a lot of pain in his chest when he breathed. He said: "This pain I feel in my chest is like a pressure.... ". His story was filled with great anguish which he could not express, but the sensation was described as painful. His body was dull; he felt tired; he could not eat properly; his eyes were filled with immense sadness. He expressed: "I can't relate to anyone in any way, not even on social media".

In the consultations, without a doubt, the feeling that came through was one of resentment, fear and pain. She always said: "I have an agony inside me that does not go away". After some time of therapy, she was able to name the feeling, she called it "father's hurts", that she could not stand the way he treated her mother. I clarify that he did not know his father. He built up a fantasy, fueled by the hurt of having been abandoned. In his imagination, his father was a rude and cruel person.

With regard to his childhood, he concludes that he was in contact with bitter factors, such as: rejection and abandonment by his father, who did not want to know him, left when he learned of his mother's pregnancy; and rejection by his mother, who accused him of being guilty of her husband's absence.

In the sessions, he did not like the "shell" technique. I use it with all my patients. This leads us to reflect that his suffering began during pregnancy, as the technique refers to the sensation of being in the mother's womb. I continued with this technique, regulating the time of application. During this period, I used the breathing technique and also "grounding", which is a rooting. After the tenth and eighth session, he was no longer feeling aversion to the "shell" technique, it became pleasant.

Rejection in the shell technique occurs when the baby suffers deprivation in pregnancy; when the first energy field, the mother's womb, is not receptive, warm and involved with the fetus. This will affect the baby's energetic condition. "If no severe damage has been inflicted in utero, the newborn brings with it a wealth of plasticity from natural development" (REICH, 1983, p. 20).

During the patient's pregnancy, the mother used substances to abort, according to her report. It is clear that his development was marked by rejection from both his father and mother. The consequence of this was the generation of a picture of emotional immaturity that was reflected in their intrapersonal and interpersonal relationships, showing resentment, bitterness and feelings of constant rejection.

Their body has blockages in the seven segments, especially the ocular, oral, diaphragmatic and pelvic. Psychological disorders are easily installed in these individuals who allow themselves to feel little or nothing.

It is in infancy, without doubt, that the factors that produce suffering, or joy, are found, because, at this time of life, the child will try to defend himself in any way possible, considering, the precarious neurological capacity of a newborn to defend himself in relation to parental rejection. This will contribute to hinder the emotional maturation of the child. In this case, the child grows up surrounded by pessimism, discouraged from promoting any recovery in favor of himself, without the right to a healthy existence. Returning to the case, after some time, his mother abandoned him and he was taken in by his sister, who was six years older than him. In other words, he was 12 and she was 18. She had become his safe haven, as he always commented at the sessions.

Thus, a child, faced with this situation, will grow up with difficulties to organize himself in life, presenting incapacities to fight, to triumph in the desired objectives. She feels she does not have some kind of merit, because the conflicting issues that have been deposited in this child go through respect, the devaluation of her rights as a human, still in formation, that is, in the mother's womb.

Therefore, it is expected that, in childhood, the child has joys, carefree, lives with freedom of tender and reciprocal expressions. This freedom is well explained by Lowen (1997) when he says that joy is not a mental process, but is born in the positive sensations of the body. These sensations come mainly from the child's relationship with the mother, still in utero. Faced with a desired pregnancy, full of joy and love, the chances of the child being healthy and born smiling will be much greater. Remembering that Spitz (1979) states that the smile is the first manifestation of health in the child. This patient did not smile and much less cried easily.

What was seen in this case, and so many others, comes up against the lack of linkage between feelings and organizing emotions of the psyche, taking refuge internally, not with joys or satisfaction, but as a defense to be able to survive. In the case of this patient, it was depression.

A lot of bodywork was done, most of the time lying down. Sometimes the work was carried out standing up, because it was evident that he had no contact with the floor, his feet were always on the armchair in the "Indian" position, that is, he showed with this posture, and from what was said, a lack of contact with reality, thus generating illusions in various aspects of his life. The more dynamic sessions, which involved the application of the "grounding" technique, were complicated, but he gradually got used to them. After eight sessions, when he arrived at the clinic, he had already taken off his shoes. After a few sessions, the patient started to talk more about his reality, cried a lot, we mourned his sister and he started to comment on a possible return to work. This awareness is common, as the technique helps the patient to connect with his body and mind, and to better understand his reality. In another moment, I started by encouraging him to express mainly his fears, his anger. Bioenergetic analysis uses some body movements that require effort, and through them patients begin to realize their tensions and their courapas.

So he nourished himself, organized himself and, after a year, happily reported his return to work. He also confided his desire to have a romantic relationship. This made me very happy, because she began to allow herself to have a social life. And it was already possible to notice a smile on his face. He tried to get closer to someone, first through social networks, then in person.

Today, after 2 years, he is still in treatment, with fortnightly sessions. He has married and they are expecting a child. Was he rushed, the reader may wonder? I would say that when we feel a little freedom and start to love ourselves, to allow ourselves, organizing our emotions, everything flows better. Fear did not disappear, but there was an understanding of its necessity. "To feel is to perceive an internal movement. If there is no movement, there is no feeling" (Lowen, 1997, p. 21). Currently, he comments: "I still feel something strange in me, but today I understand better what I feel and I know how to organize myself within it, and allow myself to have joys, to be a father, for example.... I thought I would never feel anything, because I lived like a robot, a zombie, without a floor, unable to see an inch in front of me".

Without treatment, this can lead to a situation in which the individual s prone to depression and even suicide. "If the fear or despair is too great, the person will repress all feeling, in which case the body becomes insensitive or lifeless" (Lowen, 1997, p. 20).

Another case that occurred, concerns the excessive use of negative by the patient.

The patient is 22 years old, arrived at the clinic with a medical diagnosis of severe depression.

Let's call him Antonio. He has six siblings, four of whom are unknown. In his speech, he used negatives (defense mechanism), saying: "I'm not sick"! "I don't have any depression"; "People say I'm sick, but I have nothing"; "I'm fine"; "I don't even know what I'm doing here"! Due to the way she expressed herself and acted, denying her state of health, it was very difficult to conduct her therapy and to have access to her unconscious contents. But with a lot of affection, patience and dedication, he realized his own defensive traps and understood that, if he was not sick, he was about to get sick.

I decided to leave verbal language aside and tried to concentrate on his body. For he presented a body without energy, apathetic, co orless (pall d) and rigid. After three months, with two sessions a week and many body interventions, the patient became more accessible and his painful childhood was unveiled. According to Freud, "the content of a repressed image or idea can make its way into consciousness on condition that it is denied" (Freud, 1925 - 1996, p 265). This means that the patient's denial may represent something in his unconscious, a repressed perception, which is the reverse of what is being said. Freud concludes that "this view of the negative fits very well with the fact that in analysis we never discover a 'no' in the unconscious and that the ego's recognition of the unconscious is expressed in a negative formula" (Freud, 1925-1996, p. 269).

The unconscious uses this mechanism of denial to preserve the ego from imminent danger. To accept, however, his sick condition is to attack, to unveil a repressed reality. With great caution, the patient accepted to be treated, because he realized that his condition was not healthy but sick.

Your parents were chemically dependent. His mother used marijuana, cocaine and alcohol; his father used the same substances from the age of 10. He died (was murdered) at the age of 30, in the presence of Antonio, who was 6 years old.

His parents always quarreled in his presence and, in the face of this, he always retreated into a corner and imagined he was somewhere else and with other people.

There is no doubt about the energetic deficiency in the parents' bodies, especially in the maternal uterus. Consequently, it affected Antonio's pregnancy, compromising his physical and mental formation.

In this case, the techniques of vegetotherapy were applied, which proposes a situation of neurovegetative and muscular rebalancing for each level of the body. It was also necessary to build a new uterus for the patient, which was strengthened. This is one of the proposals of the methodology within Body Psychology. According to Navarro (2013.b), vegetotherapy has the intention of releasing energetically imprisoned emotions, for this, it proposes a function of mothering the patient in order to offer what he lacked at the specific moment of life.

Antonio also has serious health problems: impaired hearing due to successive inflammations - otitis; nose and throat, with difficulty in smelling anything; bruxism; myopia; astigmatism; and visible deformities in the spine. With this, it was obvious, the blockage in the first follow-up. This blockage can be understood as a defense of the baby. "The blockage of the first level is the reaction of the newborn against the atmosphere of rejection and destructiveness that it encounters in utero or after birth" (Navarro, 2013.b, p. 30).

The first three couraga segments were worked on very hard. For

Navarro (2013.b), it is at the first level that we find the thirst for three senses (sight, hearing, smell and skin) and that these senses must be integrated, work together as soon as the baby is born, otherwise, it favors the individual to understand reality in a confused way, with distortions.

The second level, the mouth, allows the child to appropriate the environment through the function of taste and to introject or reject the environment through breastfeeding. In the case of breastfeeding, which is deficient, we have the question of orality, which favored Antonio's depressive state. We should clarify that he did not suckle at his mother's breast because she was under the effects of many drugs at the time of delivery. The child was handed over to his aunt (Antonio's father's sister), who was moved by the situation, but she did not have the psychological or financial means to adopt the child. The child was returned to his mother after three months and has remained there since his father's death.

It is in this way, when you are a child, that the happiest moments happen, or at least it should be like this, a moment of learning with an adult, with laughter, crying, respecting the natural time of the child and above all full of feelings of love. What happened in this case was the opposite of this ideal. The phrase he often said, "I don't know what I'm doing here" was interpreted and felt by me as: "I don't know what I'm doing in the world, in life and what value I have for anyone".

Lowen (1990) states that there is no more painful sensation for a child than to feel alone, lost and helpless in the world. This fear in the adult becomes less, but does not disappear.

Today, in therapy, after many movements of rescue and strengthening of his self, he has found the strength to resume a course that he had started two years before beginning the therapeutic process. Antonio is more conscious, accepting his limitations and trying to live with the health problems that still bother him.

It is therefore considered that psychopathology is a symptomatic result of a psycho-affective condition, the result of disorganized emotional energy. Thus, a healthy process in relationships from an early age leads to balance and harmony inside and outside the individual.

On the basis of what has been said so far, we can say that we become ill when we become rigid, when our organism pulsates with little intensity, when we are carriers of frozen emotions, of repressed feelings.

Among the cases attended by me, I highlight these two described above, because they served as inspiration to direct my gaze to future mothers. From them, I started to work with pregnant women, with the aim of helping them to understand their relationship with the little being in formation and thus maintain an energetic regulation between mother and baby.

9. FINAL CONSIDERATIONS

The mind has always fascinated the great scholars who spread their knowledge throughout the world, favoring the emergence of Psychology. With Freud, there was the possibility of penetrating the mystery of the human mind, although he also told us about the body. But it was with Reich that we cou d look at the human being in a more complete way (mind, body and energy), inserted in the environment and under constant pressures from that environment.

From Freud to the present day, the search for ways of understanding the mind has been progressing and, in the case of Body Psychology, it could not be otherwise, it seeks to accompany the development of the individual who, in the present times, despite the undeniable benefits offered by social and technological evolution, is in a deep state of suffering, involved in neurotic disorders, panics, deep depressions and many other tormenting pathologies of the mind. Today's conflicts, although they have the same essences as in the past, gain new dynamism and complexity.

Body Psychology, working in a simple and profound way, attentive to human suffering, brings the proposal to rescue freedom, expressiveness, reconfiguring the issues of our unconscious desires, hatrec, resentment, anguish, suffering frozen in the body, which generate displeasure, confusion, altering our perception of reality, our dreams, our way of seeing the world.

It is a new science that considers the developmental stage of the child, from gestation to adolescence, as a crucial moment for the construction of the individual's personality. In this period, the little being in development should be loved, understood and protected by the other.

In each one of us there is a desirous child who needs affection, who has fears and insecurities, but who keeps in his heart the most pressing desire to be happy and, due to the castrating prejudices and conventions imposed by today's culture, feels hindered in the realization of his ideals. In this way, the phenomenon of a rupture of homeostasis occurs, which disturbs her, physically and psychically.

In the clinical field, I am always very happy when young singles, boyfriends or even married people come to me looking for psychotherapy. Because there is a great chance of organizing themselves internally, of self-discovery and, with this, when they make a commitment to generate a child, they will be more aware and secure and, consequently, they will spare their children from a neurotic dominating and castrating action, which will harm the formation of their personality, tearing their emotional system, making them conflictive, depressive and insecure. Mannoni (1981) puts it very well that the small child is the spokesman of his parents, the symptoms manifested by him are a resonance to the anguish or the reactive processes to the anguish of his parents.

In practice, one realizes how much these anxieties have somatized in the body. Symptoms expressed verbally are often presented in a disguised form, covering up the real causes of suffering. But the body is an open book. Our body expresses what we really feel. Through it it is possible to see the truth hidden in your inner world, shaken by the traumas, the pains and afflictions that agitate your psychological core.

Body Psychology, with its precepts and techniques, teaches us to look clearly at the energetic aspects and the psychological state, that is, the spectacular magnitude of human biology and mind. The internal mechanism of the human body is wise, it guides us on which way to go to have health, the difficult thing is to be attentive to these precious tips.

In view of what has been exposed in this manuscript, we can understand that at the root of the psychic suffering of the subject today, it may have resonance with the traumas that occurred in one of the stages of his development. These traumas, in turn, are related to the lack of love that the child had to endure. The feeling of love is so important that without it, it would de-characterize the sense of beauty and life that exists in everything around us.

Paula (1994) states that love expresses the full pulse of energetic movement, involving the whole organism, as a transforming feeling of the world.

We all need affection, understanding and acceptance from others. We can say that the human being lives in function of love or is disorganized because of its absence.

In life, the search for meanings and objectives must overcome the obstacles of a fantasy reality, especially in the face of difficulties, internal conflicts. It is necessary to redirect our life towards expressiveness, towards the expansion of feelings, with rich contents, deep aspirations, such as: a return to an interrupted job; a new love relationship; the birth of a child; among other changes perceived in many cases of recovery of depressive patients, attended in recent years. With this self-perception, imbued with love, joy will soon be present and achievements will be inevitable consequences.

REFERENCES

AMERICAN PSYCHIATRIC ASSOCIATION. **Diagnostic and statistical manual of mental disorders**: DSM-5. Translation: Maria Ines Correa Nascimento, et al. 5ª ed. Porto Alegre: Artmed, 2014.

BAKER, E. F. **The human labyrinth.** Causes of the blockage of sexual energy. Sao Paulo: Summus, 1980.

BOCK, Ana M. B.; FURTADO, Odair; TEIXEIRA, MARIA L. T **Psychologies: an introduction to the study of psychology.** 13 ed. Sao Paulo: Saraiva, 2002.

REICHIAN CENTER and VOLPI.http://centroreichiano.com.br/psicologia-corporal-o-que-e/pesquisado on 30- *08-2018.*

D'ANDREA, Flavio F. **Development of personality.** 11 ed. Rio de Janeiro: Bertrand Brasil, 1994.

DAMASIO, A. R, **O Erro de Descartes:** Sao Paulo. Companhia das Letras, 1998.

DEL PORTO, Jose Alberto. Concept and diagnosis. **Rev. Bras. Psiquiatr.,** Sao Paulo, v 21, supl. 1, p. 06-11, May 1999Available   from <http://www.scielo.br/scielo.php?script=sci_arttext&pid=S1516-44461999000500003&lng=en&nrm=iso>.   access on 02 Sept. 2018.http://dx.doi.org/10.1590/S1516-44461999000500003.

FENICHEL, O. (1966). **Teoria Psicoanalitica de Las Neurosis**. Buenos Aires: Editorial Paidos.

FREUD, Sigmund. **Consciousness and what is unconscious.** In: Brazilian standard edition of the complete psychological works of Sigmund Freud, vol. XIX (1923-1925). Rio de Janeiro: Imago Editora, 1996.

FREUD, Sigmund. **On the sexual theories of children.** In: Brazilian standard edition of the psychological works of Sigmund Freud. Vol. IX. (1061908). Rio de Janeiro: Imago Editora, 1996.

FREUD, Sigmund. **Three Essays on Sexuality.** In: Brazilian standard edition of the complete psychological works of Sigmund Freud, vol. VII (19011909). Rio de Janeiro: Imago Editora, 1996.

FREUD, Sigmund. **The negative.** In: Brazilian standard edition of the complete psychological works of Sigmund Freud, vol. XIX (1923-1925). Rio de

Janeiro: Imago Editora, 1996.

FREUD, Sigmund. **Analysis of a phobia in a five-year-old boy**. In: Brazilian standard edition of the psychological works of Sigmund Freud. Vol. X. (1909). Rio de Janeiro: Imago Editora, 1996.

FREUD, Sigmund. **Pre-psychoanalytic Publications and Unpublished Essays**. In: Brazilian standard edition of the psychological works of Sigmund Freud. Vol. I. (1886-1889). Rio de Janeiro: Imago Editora, 1996.

JORGE, Marco A. C.; FERREIRA, Nadia P. **Lacan: the great Freudian.** 3 ed. Rio de Janeiro: Jorge Zahar Ed., 2009.

KAHHALE, Edna M. P. **The diversity of psychology: a theoretical construction.** Sao Paulo: Cortez, 2002.

LAPLANCHE, Jean; PONTALIS, Jean B. **Vocabulario de psicanalise.** 4 ed. Sao Paulo: Marins Fontes, 2001.

LOWEN, A. **O corpo em depressao**: as bases biologicas da fe e da realidade. Sao Paulo: Summus, 1983.

LOWEN, A. **The body in therapy**: the bioenergetic approach. Sao Pau o: Summus, 1977.

LOWEN, A. **Love, sex and your heart.** Sao Paulo: Summus, 1990.

LOWEN, A. **Bioenergetica** .5ª edigao. Sao Paulo: Summus, 1982.

LOWEN, A. **Pleasure:** A Creative Approach to Life. Sao Paulo: Summus, 1984.

LOWEN, A. **Narcissism**: Denial of the True Self. Sao Paulo: Cultrix Publishing House, 1983.

LOWEN, A. **Joy**. The surrender to the body and life. Sao Paulo: Summus, 1997.

LOWEN, A. **The rhythm of life**: a discussion of the relationship between pleasure and the noetic activities of the body; the spectrum of emotions. A hierarchy of functions, 2. 1966, new york.

MANNONI, M. **The First Interview in Psychoanalysis.** R o de Jane ro: Campus, 1981. Preface by Frangoise Dolto.

MARGIS, Regina et al. **Relationship between stressors, stress and**

anxiety. **Rev. Psychiatr. Rio Gd. Sul**. Porto Alegre, v. 25, supl. 1, p. 65-74, Apr. 2003. Available from <http://www.scielo.br/scielo.php?script=sci_arttext&pid=S0101-81082003000400008&lng=en&nrm=iso>.access
on 02 Sept. 2018.http://dx.doi.org/10.1590/S0101-81082003000400008.

MOURANO, Denise. **What is psychoanalysis for?** Rio de Janeiro: Jorge Zahar Ed., 2003.

NASIO, Juan D. **Oedipus the complex from which no child escapes.** Rio de Janeiro: Jorge Zahar Ed., 2007b.

NASIO, Juan D. **The fantasy.** Rio de Janeiro: Jorge Zahar Ed., 2007a.

NAVARRO, F. **Post-Reichian characterology.** Curitiba: Reichian Center, 2013.

NAVARRO, F. **Somatopsychopathology.** Sao Paulo: Summus, 1996.

NAVARRO, F. **Matodologia da Vegetoterapia Caractero - Analitica.** Systematics, Semiotics, Semiology and Semantics. Curitiba: Reichiano Center, 2013a.

NAVARRO, F. **Somatopsychodynamics**: reichian systematics of pathology and medical clinic. Curitiba: Reichian Center, 2013b.

NAVARRO, F. **The blockage in the 7 segments of courapa and its energetic compromises.** Article of the course of Specialization in Body Psychology. Curitiba: Reichiano Center, 2002.

WHO. **WHO definition of health**. Available at: <http://www.omsaude.com/conceito-e-definicao-de-saude-oms/>. Accessed on: 03/08/2018

PAULA, Maria Beatriz Thome. **The human being as energetic movement**. In: Energy, character and society. Rio de Janeiro: IOOR/EOLA, vol. 3, 1994, pp. 105-113.

REICH, W. **Analysis of Character.** Sao Paulo: Martins Fontes, 2009.

REICH, W. **The Function of Orgasm**. Sao Paulo: Circulo do Livro, 1975.

REICH, W. **Orgnomic Functionalism- A Journal Devoted to work of Wilhelm Reich,** vol.1 to 6, Rangeley, Maine, USA. No date.

REICH, W. **Children of the Future**: On the Prevention of Sexual Pathology.

New York: Farrar Straus Ciroux, 1983.

SELYE, H. **The Stress of Life**. New York: McGraw-Hill,'956; revised ed.,1975.

SPITZ, R. **O primeiro ano de vida.** Sao Paulo: Martins Fontes, 1983.

VOLPI, J. H. **O ambiente estressante comprometendo o desenvolvimento neuropsicofisiologico da crianga.** Curitiba: Centro Reichiano, 20C4. Available at: www.centroreichiano.com.br/artigos.htm. Accessed cn: 31/08/2018.

VOLPI, J. H.; VOLPI, S. M. **Growing up and an adventure!** Emotional development according to Body Psychology. 2ª ed. Curitiba: Centro Reichiano, 2008.

VOLPI, J. H.; VOLPI, S. M. **Reich: A Bioenergetic Analysis**. Curitiba: Cenгro Reichiano, 2003.

VOLPI, J. H. **Body Psychotherapy.** A historical path of Wilhelm Reich. Curitiba: Centro Reichiano, 2000.

VOLPI, J. H. A **memoria emocional e as somatiza^oes no corpo.** (Revista de Psicologia Corporal, vol.11) Organizers Jose Henrique Volɔi and Sandra Mara Volpi. Curitiba: Reichiano Center, 2010.

VOLPI, Sandra Mara. Psychoanalysis: a flight over the histoгy of Sigmund Freud and his ideas. Handout of the Specialization Course in Bcdy Psychology. Curitiba: Reichiano Center, 2016.

VOLPI, Jose Henrique. **Reichiana and complementary massage and vegetotherapy techniques.** Course handout. Curitiba: Reichiano Center, 2016.

VOLPI, J. H. **Body Psychotherapy:** a historical path of Wilhelm Reich. Curitiba: Centro Reichiano, 2000.

WINNICOTT, R.W. **The family and individual development**. Sao Paulo: Martins Fontes, 2013.

I want morebooks!

Buy your books fast and straightforward online - at one of world's fastest growing online book stores! Environmentally sound due to Print-on-Demand technologies.

Buy your books online at
www.morebooks.shop

Kaufen Sie Ihre Bücher schnell und unkompliziert online – auf einer der am schnellsten wachsenden Buchhandelsplattformen weltweit! Dank Print-On-Demand umwelt- und ressourcenschonend produziert.

Bücher schneller online kaufen
www.morebooks.shop

info@omniscriptum.com
www.omniscriptum.com

Printed by Books on Demand GmbH, Norderstedt / Germany